—Renwick's Portrait Studio

Hazel O'Neail was born in Nelson, B.C., and now lives in the picturesque Slocan Valley where her husband teaches school. Besides caring for her family, she finds time to do substitute teaching, to work part-time as secretary to a school principal, and to pursue her hobbies—gardening and writing, as well as her favorite sports—hiking and swimming.

Before her marriage, Mrs. O'Neail taught school in the Doukhobor settlement of Brilliant, B.C. From this stimulating experience she has drawn the hilarious incidents which comprise her sparkling little book. The colorful, uninhibited vocabulary of the Doukhobors is as much part of their characteristics as are the borsch and the kerchiefs. If their earthy language startles the reader, Mrs. O'Neail is successfully conveying the impact of their manners on a well brought up young girl.

DOUKHOBOR DAZE is her first book, but for years she has been amusing her friends with her vivid character sketches and humorous vignettes of everyday life.

To give you a glimpse of one
of our ethnic groups. I should
say one of the more picturesque.
Best Wishes for
Christmas & New Year, 1971

DOUKHOBOR

DAZE

Cover and illustrations by
Ed Cosgrove

DOUKHOBOR DAZE

BY

HAZEL O'NEAIL

go GRAY'S PUBLISHING LTD.
SIDNEY, BRITISH COLUMBIA, CANADA

Printed in Canada
by
Evergreen Press Limited
Vancouver, B.C.

First Edition - - - - - - - - - - - December, 1962
Second Edition - - - - - - - - - - - July, 1964
Third Edition - - - - - - - - - - - March, 1968

To
My young friend
NEIL
who, instead of forever badgering me with his
"Tell us about the time that . . ."
May now read it all for himself.

FOREWORD

by

FLOS JEWELL WILLIAMS

The Doukhobors, a persecuted peasant minority, came to Canada sixty years ago from Trans-Caucasia, almost within view of Mount Ararat. They brought strange customs and patterns of behaviour with them which in the extreme resulted in burning of homes, bombing of bridges and schools and parading in the nude when local laws conflicted with their religious beliefs. There are two groups, the law-abiding Orthodox Doukhobors and the troublemakers, the fanatical Sons of Freedom.

This is the story of a young girl who went from school to teach among these strange people some 25 years ago. The scene is set in the mountainous interior of British Columbia and is a personal account of how she faced danger with courage, difficulties with gaiety and frustrations with a highly developed sense of humor.

SEPTEMBER

WEDNESDAY, SEPTEMBER 4

> *"The pen of the author and statesman*
> *Shall be held in a little brown hand."*

THAT'S what THEY told us at Normal School, their voices quivering with timbre and verve. I wonder if they meant the author of all the four-letter words I have just found chalked on the walls of the boys' privy out back? Every obscene word I have ever heard is there, as well as some unknown, to me at least. Maybe these mysterious ones are not words at all, but they *look* like bad characters. Of course, even "floor" or "walk" would smirk suggestively in this gathering—which just goes to show what environment can do.

So this is Pleasant! This stark, grey structure squatting on the bald, treeless prairie! This desolate, dust-covered shelf in the hills! But the inspector said I'd been assigned to School Pleasant, three miles from Brilliant station, two hundred yards off the righthand side of the road—so—this must be Pleasant. There is another school about a mile farther on, at what is called Ootischenia, but there is no doubt that this is my destination.

But how different this spot is from the tree-shaded valley through which I came just a short while ago! Back along the flat, down the hill, and around the bend, the country

1

is a Shangri-la, with bright, green grass even now, full-skirted shrubs and bushes, and patchwork-quilt orchards surrounding the red brick villages. Up here, on the second bench above the noiselessly-gliding jade Columbia, prairie seems to have taken over along one side of the road, for there are endless flat wheat fields crowding and pushing their relentless way right up to the very door of the school-room. They are only expanses of dry bristle now, with inches of powdery earth covering them; even to step gingerly on it raises clouds of white dust which stifle one. The road, ankle-deep in dust, stretches straight and unimaginative between two double rows of power lines, and goes on and on into the shimmering distance as far as the eyes can reach. Across the road are scrawny, neglected-looking orchards hugging the villages, which are spaced a half-mile or so apart.

There is not a tree anywhere near the school, and I wonder what it will be like in June, when old Sol glares down hour after hour, with nothing to break his burning assault. Pleasant, wot?

Later: Report on schoolroom and living quarters:— former, a fairly large room containing thirty-eight desks, ranging in size from unbelievably tiny to monstrously large; a desk and chair for me; and a water bucket (grimy). Living quarters:—a kitchen-living-room boasting a table, two straight chairs, one ragged wicker armchair, a cupboard, a camp stove, a water bucket (grimy) enthroned on an apple box under a verdigris encrusted tap, and a small assortment of dishes and utensils. Near the stove, a trap door opens to reveal a dark hole in the earth's nether regions. There is also a bedroom furnished with a squeaky-springed, lumpy-mattressed bed, a dresser, and a tiny heater, whose name appears to be "Queen". That is all that is in the place —except for the strangest musty smell throughout. Pleasant? Hah!

From my windows, I can see the everlasting fields, and here and there, a "village". Every unit of two Doukhobor houses is called a village, each accommodating two families with its amazing collection of grandparents and in-laws of

2

every conceivable age. The Doukhobors call themselves "The Christian Community of Universal Brotherhood," but how people can live in a jumble like this, and still be either Christians or brothers, is a quandary to me.

The villages are all identical in shape and size, but occasionally a house is wooden, unpainted and weatherbeaten, instead of the usual red brick. No slightest attempt has been made to beautify them; there are no formal walks, no flower beds, no paint, no curtains at the windows. At the back of each pair of houses is a low wooden structure shaped like an elongated, inverted U; this building, with the inside walls of the two main houses, forms a sort of courtyard where scores of children scream and fight, and as many mothers, grandmothers, and aunts holler and argue. Behind each village is a conglomeration of unpainted, rickety barns, sheds, shacks, privies, and huts of every size and description.

Have just inspected the school register — but how can this *be?* Abrossimoff, Babakaoff, Chernenkoff, Davidoff, Fofanoff, Gevatkoff, Harasimoff, Kabatoff, Katelnikoff, Koftinoff, Konkin, Koochin, Laverenchinkoff, Nichivelodoff, Perepelkin, Pictin, Popoff, Rezansoff, Sherstibitoff, Stoochnoff, Stooshnoff, Stoopnikoff, Veregin, Wasilenkoff, Zaitsoff, Zoobkoff—I'm bewilderedoff!

And that's not all. There are three Petes, three Johns, three Mikes, three Fannies, two Tenas, three Marys, three Nicks, two Pollys, three Annies, four Bills. This could become very confusing, so—I shall change their names thus: Pete, Peter, and Pat; John, Johnny, and Jack; Mike, Michael, and Mickey; Fannie, Flora, and Florence; Tena and Tannis; Mary, Marion, and Marie; Nick, Nicholas, and Nicky; Polly and Pauline; Annie, Anne, and Annette; Bill, Billy, Will, and Willie. So be it.

Now for some supper. I have three cups of water which have gathered in the bucket in the past two hours—with the faucet turned full on! None of your gushing, city-slicker water pressure here, I can see. This tap drips once every four-and-a-half seconds. In order to wash dishes *and* myself tonight, I should have arrived here a week earlier, and spent the intervening time garnering these precious drops.

3

Well, I won't leave dirty dishes anyway; as to myself, dish-water may have to suffice.

Midnight: Have worked all evening unpacking and preparing an opening program for tomorrow. This place at night is the original Chamber of Horrors—not because of noise—but because of the eerie stillness, broken only by the mournful howling of a dog somewhere in the distance. C-c-could it be a werewolf? There is not a glimmer of light anywhere. There is just me, suspended in this weird nothingness, in this . . . this . . . Pleasant! Why is it that absence of sound is more frightening than the crack of doom? Have I the courage to go out to the you-know-what? Or could I maybe convince myself that Nature does not call? Well? Could I? Hm? . . . (oh, go on, y' big sissy).

I d-d-d-did!

THURSDAY, SEPTEMBER 5

The first day's session is over. My pupils began arriving in bare-footed droves at 8 a.m. The High Potentates at Normal School made it very clear that on the first day of school, any self-respecting teacher would be in her classroom before any of her young hopefuls appeared on the scene. There you must be, they said, glowing and sparkling with sweetness and light, emitting rays of enthusiasm and zeal. (Popping like a blasted neon sign, sounded like!)

So there I was. I tried to do as I had been taught, and maybe I succeeded, at least in part. But I would very much like to see what my instructor in School Administration would look like after six hours of lying in a torture-rack like my bed is, listening and waiting for heaven knows what horror to descend upon him. *He'd* have blue hammocks of cornstarch-pudding consistency under *his* eyes too, I betcha!

I have ten classes, from Primary to Grade 8, and thirty-eight pupils whose ages range from five to fourteen. The five-year-old Tena Rezansoff I am not obliged to enroll, but her mother brought her and beseeched, "And you will take dis Tena.? Now even at home I got t'ree more keeds, and here's too myany noise. And you will take?"

So I took. As Mrs. Rezansoff left, I heard someone say, "And already she got five keeds, and now again she will get. E-h-h, sawme kinda cryazy!" (Check).

My class recited The Lord's Prayer this morning, but it sounded very strange, so later I gave paper to the older pupils and asked them to write the prayer. This was one result:

Our father bedart in heaven hello bedie name. Die king come die willie done in earth as it is in heaven. Give us this day our delly bread in forgive us our trespers as we forgive those who tresper against us. And lid us not in two temtion but diliver us from eevil for dine is the king come the power and the glory forever and ever all men.

Followed the writing of the prayer on the blackboard, by me, and an explanation of each part. Said Alec Gevatkoff, in great surprise, "And Meess Hulls, we didn't know it *means* sawmetheeng!"

I made a record of their ages. When I came to Mike Perepelkin, he said that he was nine, and his birthday January seventh. Pete Perepelkin stated that he was Mike's brother, his age also nine, and his birthday April twentieth.

5

"One of you must be mistaken," I said. "You can't both be nine. One of you must be either eight or ten. Or perhaps you have your birthdates wrong."

"No, Meess Hulls, and I am nine, and Mike is nine," replied Pete.

"Yes, Meess Hulls, and I am nine, and Pete is nine," chirped Mike.

Knowing that they were confused somehow, I instructed them to ask at home, and to bring me their correct ages and birthdates after lunch. They came back with the information that Mike is definitely nine and born on January seventh, and that Pete is also just as definitely nine, and born on April twentieth. Of the same year! Well, maybe so, but this didn't conform with what I've heard about the bees and flowers. I sent them home after school, each with a slip of paper inscribed thus:

Pete Perepelkin, age   .
Birthdate   , year   .
Mike Perepelkin, age   .
Birthdate   , year   .

Apparently they couldn't wait until to-morrow to prove that they had been correct, for in a very short while they came whooping over the stubble, waving their bits of paper. The information thereon was that Mike was nine on January seventh, and Pete was nine on April twentieth—*of the same year!*

This was amazing! I was wondering whether I should dash off a telegram to some medical journal when Mike drawled. "And whyen I was small, I stayed wit' Pete's mawder for a long time because mawder-my been vyery seeck."

"What did you say, Mike?" I asked, sensing that I was perhaps on the track of an explanation at last.

"And mawder-my been seeck, and Pete's mawder been looking after me."

"Haven't you and Pete the same mother?"

6

They both howled with laughter at this very amusing question, and Mike said, "No, and Pete got his mawder, and I got mine."

"But you said that you and Pete were *brothers!*"

"And shure, Meess Hulls, and we are. We are bot' cawsin-brawders!"

"And yes," echoed Pete, "Shure we are brawders! We are cawsin-brawders wit' Mike."

Now it was Pete and Mike who were baffled—at my ignorance. After all—cousins, brothers, wives—what's the difference?

This is just a case of history repeating its maddening self. It is a junior version of the sort of ridiculous palaver which, in the trials of suspected arsonists, exasperates the courts, and starts judges gnashing their teeth and tearing their hair. Last summer in Nelson, prior to the evacuation of 592 Sons of Freedom to Piers Island Penitentiary, the hearings were prolonged day after tedious day owing to just such entanglements as mine of today. In one instance, the stand was occupied by a woman who was being questioned in connection with the burning of a house. The case proceeded in this vein:

"Were you present when this house was burned?"

"And yes, and I was dere."

"Did you go into the house?"

"And yes, and I was going in lawtsa times."

"But did you go in before the fire?"

"Shure. I was going in dot house lawtsa times."

"Did you go in *immediately* before the fire?"

"Shure."

"Were you carrying anything when you went in?"

"And yes, I was carrying sawmetheeng."

(Hah! Now we're getting somewhere; she's going to admit entering the house carrying coal oil or gasoline!)

"What were you carrying when you went into the house?"

"My arms and legs."

7

Replies like this are regular stock-in-trade with these people. The simplest, most direct question, whether it be, "Did you burn this house?" or "How much do you charge for potatoes?" invariably catapults the interrogator into the most maddening situations. And what's more, they always seem to get the best of it ultimately. Whether they are so exasperating through STUpidity, or CUpidity, I don't know.

Night seems to be the Doukhobors' time to howl. The young people wander up and down the road in groups, giving forth the most mournful, dirge-like singing. It is really more chanting than singing, and has a peculiar grating cacophony, in spite of bits of harmony here and there. It sounds more weird from a little distance than at close range, and is as eerie to awaken to, in the night, as the long whine of a coyote, or the scream of a cougar. I may be wrong, but it sounds as though the voices are accompanied by the howls of souls in torment, and the wails of banshees.

FRIDAY, SEPTEMBER 6

Girded up my loins this morning, and descended through the trap door to look over the situation down there. I *hate* cellars. Basements are fine—but these horrible, lightless, little caverns festooned with arcs of cobwebs and encrusted with shiny snail tracks give me the creeps. I did find one treasure, though—another tap. And this one produces water in the traditional way, not just in stingy little drops. Whee! Now I can wash both hands every day.

On the south wall of my kitchen there is a large ugly spot where, at some time in the past, the plaster has broken and fallen out, so at noon I asked my pupils if there was anyone who could patch it for me. Someone said that a John Nichivelodoff could "plyaster" and I sent word for him to come round and do it whenever convenient for him. This is very odd plaster; it has what seem to be bits of straw or grass in it, just under the finishing coat, and is a peculiar color, neither white nor yellow nor grey, but a combination of all three.

Old John, laden with bucket and trowel, came shuffling over the fields right on the nose of three o'clock. He is a hollow-eyed, flat-cheeked, pale green specimen who looks as though he had just crawled out from under a stone. He curled up his lip in a grin, exposing three yellow fangs, and cheerfully announced, "And now I wyill pyaster sawn-ofabeetch hole."

As he slathered his trowel around in the bucket, and applied the plaster in slupping blobs, I asked him what it was that had been put on the walls before the final coat.

"Oh," he wheezed, wiping his long, blue nose on his shirt sleeve, "and dot's cowshyit. Make plyaster styick vyery good."

? ! ! ! ?

He went on, "And some guy tell me fawder-your is con-tryactor for byuilding houses, huh? Dot's right?" and when he had my affirmative reply, he continued, "And you askit fawder-your might he would need plyastering myan. I am vyery good for plyaster vork. Like me nobody can ply-aster. You askit fawder-your."

"Wel-ll," I faltered, "I think he has his regular plaster-ers and wouldn't need anyone right now."

"No myatter, you askit. And he need, I weel go," John announced, with the air of one bestowing a very great favor. He was soon finished, and now I knew what the stale, musty odor was! Truly, it's an ill wind. . . . With a final grin, and a last reminder to "askit fawder-your" he left, slam-ming the door behind him, and plop! out fell the new plaster in a soggy heap on the floor. As I cleaned up the gritty mess, I couldn't help wondering how Dad would sound as he displayed his newest house and said, with a flourish, "And this room, Mrs. Vandersnoot, is done in the latest cow-manure-scented plaster."

SUNDAY, SEPTEMBER 8

Sunday evening. Have just returned from Nelson, and a most delightful week-end. Dad does NOT need a plasterer.

Several of my pupils were here to greet me when I arrived. I felt like a broken-down freight truck after stag-gering and floundering the three miles from the bus

9

loaded down with two suitcases, one packed with canned goods. Wish I could subsist on feathers—they'd be so much lighter to carry.

The youngsters, in a tizzy of excitement, helped me un-pack, and kept up a steady chatter that made them sound like flustered chickens. It was all very cosy and jolly until Anne Fofanoff threw in her two-bits' worth, her eyes round with anxiety, "And Meess Hulls, aren't you afraid to stay here all by yourself at night?"

(Wh-h-o, m-m-me?)

Steadying all my quivering bones, I literally forced my heart to pump some more of its frigid jelly through my veins as I croaked, "A-f-fraid? Wh-what would I b-be af-f-fraid of? Heh-heh, of course not, Anne. Why do you ask that?"

She glanced over her shoulder into the dusk, and replied, "And I don't know, Meess Hulls, but mawder-my and gran'-mawder, too, dey every time say dey wouldn't stay all alone, and I wouldn't, too. I t'eenk byetter now we go home. Eet weell dark soon. Good-bye, dear Meess Hulls. I am vyery sorry for you to stay here all by yourself."

Arms linked, they wavered off into the shadows, leaving me to stand there listening . . . listening. Good heavens, if even the women who had lived here all their lives were nervous . . . what of me, to whom all this was strange? What of me, who had never before spent a night alone, in my whole life? What . . ? How . . ? And then I heard it . . . a dull BUMP - BUMP! In the gathering dusk, it came to me, strangely, stranglingly close . . . BUMP - BUMP! I eyed the trap door, and knew at once where the Fiend was hiding. As quietly as I could, I hauled my table and chair over on top of it, and prepared to sit there till morning— if the fates willed that I should survive until the beautiful, beautiful morning. I tried to set my mind to planning lessons for to-morrow — BUMP - BUMP! — not that to-morrow would matter much, in view of what might befall me at any time now. But if I sat there, at least I'd know when HE started to come up with either a cleaver in his hand, or rape in his eye. Dear God, I silently prayed, let

10

it be quick—and not too gory! I waited, and listened . . . and there it was, as before — BUMP!-BUMP! Oh why, I wailed in my soul, did I ever take up teaching? BUMP! Why hadn't I just become a clerk in Woolworth's, surrounded by the lovely, musical clang of cash registers and hundreds of wonderful, cranky customers? BUMP!-BUMP! Why hadn't I hired out as a chambermaid? Why, oh why hadn't I married that what's-his-name last year? BUMP!-BUMP! Or gone into a monastery—no, a convent? Or *anything* but this! Holy saints, I'd even jump in with old John Nichivelodoff right now, just for company. . . .

And then, right then, I noticed a peculiar lurching movement under my sweater! And that's where the BUMP!-BUMP! was coming from—from under my sweater, for heaven's sake!

And this is only Sunday night! Four more nights, after this one, before the weekend. This is only September. Three more months, with the dark closing in earlier and earlier every day, before Christmas vacation. But what am I worrying about? I'll be all safe and warm in a lovely, lovely padded cell long before then. Oh happy, happy day!

MONDAY, SEPTEMBER 9

It's morning, and nothing crawled up out of the cellar, but I sat on that accursed trap door until 1.30 a.m. just the same. By that time, the wailing out on the road had shrunk into stillness, and the awful quiet had seeped into my brain where it swirled and roared in its immensity. I crept into bed, shivering and perspiring at the same time, and I must even have slept, because at seven I came out of some sort of coma to find my hands still as tightly clenched as when I had silently eased my aching joints, and throbbing head, onto that varicose-veined mattress.

In a health lesson to Grade two this morning, I was trying to put across the value of deep breathing—(I, who haven't drawn a full breath since I came out here!) I told the class to place their hands on their ribs, take a good deep breath, and feel how their inflating lungs expanded the ribs. They all followed instructions, swallowing and gasping and

11

gulping, and then up popped Johnny Laverenchinkoff with, "And you know, Meess Hulls, gran'mawder-my hyave how BEE-E-EG longs! Down to her stawmick dey hyang!"

Nearly all the Doukhobor women are very well upholstered in all sections. Obesity seems to be a criterion of beauty, and even the young women make no attempt to control their tendency to fatness, nor even to mould it into curves. They are all soft and ploppy; and everything, fore and aft, jiggles as they walk. Even their full blouses and voluminous skirts do not conceal the quiverings and lurchings of these regions of their anatomies. One of these skirts, spread out, would make a tent almost large enough to shelter a good-sized revival meeting. Everyday ones are made of flowered print, the gaudier the better, but dress-up ones are silk, often fearful in hue, and trimmed with lace, tucks, or ribbon, and often a combination of all three. Over the skirt is worn an apron, also silk, and in a color which screams as hideously as possible with the tint of the skirt. The blouse is a shapeless affair with plain round neck, long gathered sleeves, and vertical tucks from throat to waist, and made, of course, in a color that goes one farther than that of the apron. Stockings are knit from coarse homespun wool, dyed usually a snarling pink, a shrieking bluish-green, or a nightmarish orange. A "plutok" completes the ensemble; this is a head shawl, generally soft white cashmere or heavy white silk, beautifully embroidered, by hand, with exquisite pink roses, and trimmed with silk fringe.

There is nothing on earth as colorful (nor as cruel to the eyes) as the sight of a bevy of Doukhobor women parading along the road in their Sunday regalia. The men are very orthodox in their attire except for an occasional shirt or pair of socks in the same loud pink, blue, or orange as the women's stockings.

TUESDAY, SEPTEMBER 10

Bathing in the wilds is a venture which should be undertaken only by a superhuman being, endowed with unlimited resourcefulness and ingenuity, and a great store of patience. First of all, you burn up all of to-morrow's wood in heating the water you lugged up from the cellar. Then you draw all the blinds down, and thumb-tack the torn edges to the window frames. Now you bring in the galvanized tub and, in filling it, you spill two-thirds of the water on the floor, leaving approximately four saucersful in which to bathe. You step into the tub. So far, so good. But since the thing measures about two feet in diameter, sitting down in it entails considerable headwork—and seatwork! If you try to cross your ankles, there is no room left in which to get at the water, and after all, you didn't go to all this trouble just to sit. So you uncross your ankles and plant your feet squarely on the bottom of the tub. Ah, that's better. But when you reach forward to the water, you gouge your left eye with your left knee. No better from the other side. If you go at it sideways, you knock your left eye with your right knee, and vice versa; so if you don't devise some other system, you can't hope to get out of this without one shiner at least. Maybe if you hung your feet outside the tub? No good: too cold, too much slop, and too uncomfortable. You pull your feet in again. Ho hum, what now? Let's see; perhaps if you put your feet together, and let your knees veer off in opposite directions? Yes, that's the best yet. Of course, by this time the water is cold, but you're so steamed up from all the gymnastics that you don't mind cooling off a bit. When you get to your back, you discover that the water all runs down outside the tub, but there are only a few spoonsful left in the bottom now anyway, so what's the difference?

You're finished. You cart out what remains of the water, and the tub. You wipe up the floor. You wait for the refreshed feeling that always follows a bath—but it doesn't come. Instead, you're worn to a frazzle from so much physical endeavour, and mentally exhausted as a result of all the brainwork this performance required. Nuts! You'll go dirty from now on.

WEDNESDAY, SEPTEMBER 11

Last night and the night before, I worked till all hours on school lessons. This means preparing oral lessons

13

for each grade, as well as "busy-work" for all who are not scheduled for a teaching class. At Normal we made ducky timetables which took care of everybody every moment of the day—theoretically—and looked simply stunning in their perfection. What was not anticipated was the fact that in a class like this, there are a number of shining lights who have completed their busy-work in forty seconds flat, and another group of tortoises who never finish one single assignment in a whole day of prodding. The bright ones then proceed to be a darn nuisance because of their idleness, and the slow ones sit chewing their pencils and gazing at nothing. A teacher in an ungraded school could never be accused of having a single-track mind, because while she jabs at the blackboard and gabbles on and on in her teaching lesson, she simultaneously harps at the dawdlers and pleads with the quick ones to "find some other work to do."

Nor did they know at Normal that there are places where the beginners do not understand one word of English. Let's see some of those lofty instructors tackle that one.

The preparation of seatwork is accomplished night after night with the aid of a hectograph pad. This is a devilish contraption which some perverted fiend sat up all night to devise. First you buy gelatine and glycerine (with your own money which you haven't got any of yet, because you don't get your first cheque until on in October). You melt these together and then pour the resulting mess onto a cookie sheet, being careful not to let any bubbles form on the surface—which they do by the hundreds. Then you hang maternally over the thing, scooping off the blasted bubbles. When it has cooled and set, it is a half-inch-thick rubbery sheet which resembles the sponge cake I made last week. Now you draw, print, and write things with a purple concoction known as hectograph ink. The master copy is laid on the pad, pressed firmly onto it for a few seconds to set the original drawing or writing, and then it is pried off. Now several sheets may be duplicated. Once used for a copy, the pad must stand for a couple of days to allow this impression to soak into the jelly; or you can scrub at it immediately with soap and water to remove the ink. This takes much scrubbing and many bad thoughts about the enchantress at Normal who gave you this infernal formula with the attitude that she was handing over the crown jewels. To add a little spice to the procedure, you can, for a change, sometimes use *green* hectograph ink. In any case, when you are through cleaning the pad eleven times each night, your hands are dyed deep lavender or pale jade, neither of which can be removed by anything on earth save time, or perhaps lye—if it were applied in a solution strong enough to peel off layers one, two, and three of your precious hide. Your arms, ears, the end of your nose, and one eyebrow are also invariably streaked with these delightful tints, making you look like a circus clown three minutes before he has completed his makeup. To the wretch who invented the hectograph pad and its trappings, I can only say this: how I'd love to boil you in a cauldron filled to the brim with your own odious goo! Still, how to manage without it? Not for us, apparently, the gilded mimeograph machines that are standard equipment in town schools.

THURSDAY, SEPTEMBER 12

It was a glorious morning and, as I thought, a fine time to take my class out for some brisk physical jerks. I was surprised to find that they understood none of the commands such as, "stand at ease", "attention", "hips firm", etc., nor the rhythm of arm exercises to counting. I was deep in instruction along these lines, and had them on the verge of coming smartly to attention, when I spied old Pete Derhousoff coming across the field with a purposeful stride. From shouting distance he roared, "Wot you do here?" I waited until he came up to me and then unsuspectingly said, "Good morning, Mr. Derhousoff. We're having some exercises."

"Wyell, you stawpit doing like dot," he growled menacingly. I was puzzled and asked, "But why? It's good for the children to have exercises out in the fresh air."

"And I say you stawpit! You t'eenk you gonna make soldiers for our cheeldren, and Dou'hobors don't want no soldiers."

"But Mr. Derhousoff," I tried to reason, "this is part of their education, just like reading and writing. It helps to make healthy boys and girls."

He sucked in his breath, grew almost purple with rage, and shook his grimy fist under my nose as he bellowed, "And stawpit, I tyell you! Dou'hobors don't want no soldiers! And you don't stawpit, I gonna tyell gawverment!"

So—I guess setting up exercises are military training, and will have to be replaced by ring games. I wonder if previous teachers learned the fact in this same way? No doubt the children were enjoying themselves too much to warn me of what would inevitably happen. Of course this is why they knew none of the commands; they have not been allowed to do formal jerks.

There is no flag here, either, for the flag-raising ceremony common to all other schools. That, too, would certainly come under the heading of militarism.

The past three nights have been just as nerve-wracking as all the others. Groups of boys and young men seem to be forever on the prowl around the school, especially after dark. Perhaps they are trying to work up the courage to come visiting me, I don't know.

The horrible chanting goes on and on, every night, until I wish that I were deaf so that I could remove my hearing-aid and not have to listen to it. I have now reached the stage where my nerves are all dangling outside my clothes, and to have even a blade of grass brush me after 4 p.m. sets them all a-tingle. I have caught myself babbling incoherently on one or two occasions, and no doubt the time will have come for me to entrain for a mental home when I discover saliva dripping off my chin. My chief dread right now is that others will notice it before I do, and walk in circles around me, whispering (loudly enough for me to hear), "The poor thing! She should be Put Away."

FRIDAY, SEPTEMBER 13

My abode is overflowing with plums—red plums, blue plums, purple plums, yellow plums, ripe plums, green plums, big plums, little plums, middle-sized plums—EVERY-body brings me plums, and I abhor plums. Apples are crunchy; peaches are luscious; pears are juicy; strawberries are delicious;—but plums—well, plums just haven't a thing. And here I am, about to be buried alive in the insipid things!

MONDAY, SEPTEMBER 16

Have decided, apropos of instructions at Normal, that in spite of the fact that it will mean I'll have to work later than ever at night, I'd better steal an hour or so after school, once or twice a week, and make a few calls at the homes of some of my pupils. Accordingly, I hied me forth into the blue-and-gold afternoon, and headed for the Stoopnikoff village, which sprawls untidily under the brow of the hill rising from this bench to another just above. It was a jaunt of perhaps half a mile, and I'd forgotten how truly lovely it can be outdoors in September. A little fresh air is a wonderful tonic for that down-at-the-mouth feeling, and I even found myself beginning to think that I didn't really mind Brilliant so much after all. (Except for the nights, and I refused to bend over backwards pretending that I liked those!)

I met a hunched old woman trailing along the road beside two wall-eyed, tail-switching cows, knitting as she hobbled through the dust, while the meandering animals nibbled at the dry, brown weeds. (The grandparents seemingly having outlived any other usefulness, tend the cattle day in and day out, and may be seen at any time patiently shuffling along behind a cow or two). She gave me a shrivelled, toothless grin, bowed, and murmured, "Slava hospidi."

As I turned in at the Stoopnikoff gate, Nellie, Fannie and young Paul came hurtling through the burnt grass to meet me, and proudly escorted me to the back door of their home. We entered the huge kitchen where three women, wearing their everyday plutoks even on this warm day, sat peeling and quartering apples. These would later replace the wizened ones I had noticed scattered on raised screens out in the courtyard, where they are placed in the sun to dry—and also to be buzzed over, and squatted upon, by a million-odd flies. Fannie pointed to each of the women in

17

turn and enumerated them as her mother, aunt, and grand-mother. None of them could speak English, but their broad smiles and low bows of greeting made me feel that I was more than welcome. Conversation was carried on by means of the children's interpretation and many gestures.

The room was large and cheerless, the only furnishings (besides another zooming, angry horde of flies) being a very long table and two benches roughly, but sturdily, made, a huge black cookstove with a set of shelves behind it, and a wide bench-like table beside the heavy galvanized sink. There were no curtains, and no covering on the rough, uneven floor. In one corner, behind and to the right of the stove, the chimney had been extended sideways, forming an almost-square brick box, with an opening covered by a piece of zinc. Mrs. Stoopnikoff rose at that moment, re-moved the zinc "door", and inserted a long pole with a wire-hooked end into the hole. Immediately she hauled it out again, and on the hook was the most colossal loaf of bread that I have ever seen. It was round, measuring fully four-teen inches in diameter, and six or eight inches in height. Again and again she went fishing, until she had seven of these monstrous loaves on the table. I then inspected the oven and discovered that the bread is baked right on the brick floor. Fannie explained that a very hot fire is built in the oven very early in the morning, and after it has burned completely away, the ashes are raked out and the loaves put in without benefit of pans.

With this chore finished, Mrs. Stoopnikoff said some-thing to Nellie, who then asked me, "And Meess Hulls, mawder-my say you would like to see our house?" I had thought that this was their house, but followed them all out the door to another door in the long, low building at the back. We entered a room which was obviously a bedroom, (so "house" must mean "bedroom"), with another adjoin-ing it on either side, each with its own entrance from out-side. Each contained one or two beds covered with home-made, wool-filled comforters, several chairs, a small heater, and various small stools and tables. At the foot of the bed in the centre of the room, suspended on ropes from a hook in the ceiling, hung an unpainted wooden box, measuring approximately four by two and a half feet, and about a foot deep. This was the cradle, no less! When little Pete or Polly awakens yowling in the night, ma or pa simply disengages a foot from the blankets, reaches out, and sends

Junior whooshing rhythmically back and forth. The yowling ceases, and parents haven't trod one step on the cold floor. (I shall make a note of this ingenious invention against the day when I may have offspring).

19

There were several rugs on the floors which Nellie said her mother had made from old clothing cut in strips, dyed, braided, and then sewn round and round into these oval mats.

We then proceeded to the front room of the main building. It opened directly off the kitchen and was very large, and entirely devoid of anything in the way of comfort, since it contained only a table, a heater, and a large number of straight chairs and benches. This room, Fannie explained, is used only for weddings and funerals. There was a hallway outside, with a staircase leading to eight small rooms upstairs, four on each side of a long, narrow corridor. These are "houses", usually occupied by older sons and daughters.

That is the layout of each of these houses, so large and barren looking, both inside and out. BUT—the delightful perfume of Attar of Cowmanure pervades this place just as enchantingly as it does Pleasant! Be it ever so humble . . . (or smelly!) . . .

TUESDAY, SEPTEMBER 17

Well, last night and the night before passed uneventfully (for which Allah be praised!) except for one small detail: I came to, at about 3 a.m. this morning to find that . . . I was not . . .alone . . .IN MY BED!

Some sound must have awakened me from a deep sleep. I raised my right arm up over my head to adjust my pillow and—oh no! . . . NO! But it was! It WAS! . . . I . . . oh, dear God, I . . . felt . . . FLESH! . . . human f-f-flesh . . . right alongside my head, on the left side! All my blood congealed—except the pint that had already started through my heart, and it plunked on in icy chunks. With what little strength I had left, I gingerly touched IT again—to make SURE I wasn't just having a bad dream. It was no dream; it really *was* flesh! It couldn't be. But it was!! Just before my toes curled up, and before my heart ceased to function, I decided to p-p-push on the Thing. I was a dead cinch to expire anyway, but not without an attempt, how-

20

ever feeble, to oust this . . . this . . . THAT, with its c-c-cold, c-c-cold flesh.

Since IT was on my left, I thought hysterically that I could maybe push better with that hand, thus saving any jiggling of the bed and therefore any warning to the Thing, that I had wakened. Cautiously, I prepared to get ready to begin to commence to start p-p-pushing. But—but—but I couldn't *find* any left hand! I simply no longer *had* a left hand ! Not even the stump ! Oh holy saints ! Could I have been injected with something, and had my arm cut off without my knowing it? But—surely, then, there'd be b-b-blood?? And why, oh WHY was IT so still? . . .

Suddenly, unbelievably, blessedly—I began to feel a peculiar tingling sensation where my left arm—my beautiful, beautiful left arm—should have been! And oh, dear diary, it was there! MY LEFT ARM WAS THERE! As it prickled agonizingly back to glorious life, I lay in a puddle of perspiration and realized that I'd dozed off with it awkwardly twisted above my head and it, as well as I, had been asleep!

I know now that I was in the last stage of Death from Fright. I shall never be convinced that rigor mortis did not place its clammy paw upon me in that terrifying moment when I first felt that horrible, cold, cold flesh. So I have discovered something which should be of value to the medical profession, i.e., even rigor mortis can be cured, if it is caught in time!

FRIDAY, SEPTEMBER 20

I had Tannis Wasilenkoff in for a little while after school to-day. Tannis has dark olive skin, black hair, and the deepest brown eyes I have ever seen. When she smiles, she is mischievous imp personified; a deep, crescent dimple nestles then at the corner of her mouth, and her eyes flash and dance merrily. But Tannis is not always light-hearted, and many times I have seen her sitting at her desk with a far-away look in those beautiful eyes. She sat thus to-day, thinking and brooding, so I asked her if there was something troubling her. She nodded her head and I said,

"Would you like to tell me about it, Tannis?" Her eyes filled with great crystal tears and her voice trembled as she sobbed, "Oh-h-h Meess Hulls! And I want so moch an Eenglish dryess! I don't want to wyear dis Doukhobor clodes! And I *hyate* Doukhobor dryesses!"

I knew that my reply was inadequate, even before I voiced it. But I said, "Well, Tannis—then you would be different from all the other girls. Don't you think it's better if you all dress alike?"

Tears spilled down her cheeks as she shook her head. "No, Meess Hulls. I weesh I could hyave just wan Eenglish dryess—just only *wan!*"

My heart ached for her in her longing. I pictured how adorable she would look in a starched, frilly pink or yellow organdy—or even crisp gingham, and I longed to tell her that I would make her dream come true. But of course I could not. It isn't possible for me to single out one pupil for a gift . . . is it . . . ? No—not even when that course would fulfill a little girl's most cherished dream.

I sent Tannis home with a pink ribbon in her hair, her eyes dried . . . and the longing for wan Eenglish dryess still in her heart. For me? A big lump in my throat.

5:30 *p.m.* — another week is finished and I'm ready to leave for home. I have before me a whole delightful weekend of basking under electric lights, soaking (stretched out at full length) in a real, honest-to-goodness bathtub, and rubbing elbows with all the lovely, lovely friends who ladle sympathy over me like syrup and say, "It's simply criminal that a young girl should have to live like that—no lights! no water! no sanitary facilities! no company! no protection! no nothing! And my dear, aren't you terribly nervous out there amongst those dreadful people?"

I lap it up, and am very brave and nonchalant—while I'm in town!

SUNDAY, SEPTEMBER 22

Had a terrific struggle with the gas lamp tonight. The gas lamp is another brainchild of the same machiavellian devil who came up with the hectograph pad. To light one of these products of the underworld requires a set of cast-iron nerves, the patience of the Sphinx, the daring of Buffalo Bill, and a vocabulary entirely devoid of any knowledge of profanity. I do not qualify, so the lamp is sheer anathema to me.

First, you fill the beastly thing, sloshing gas all over everything since the addle-pated inventor cunningly made the bowl out of nickel or something, through which it is impossible to see the level of the fuel within until it is too late. Now you hunt for the pump—a silly little brother to a tire pump—and when you have finally located it under the bed, or behind the kindling, you pump like mad into a little ear in the lampbowl, which you make by untwisting a screw which is always stuck. When you are exhausted, and can't make it take one more puff, you have to quickly wind the screw back in, only there's no use, because while you lay the pump down, all the stinking air comes gushing out with a loud s-s-sfsh! and you're right back where you started. (This is where the vocabulary comes in.) After five of these manoeuvres, you finally succeed in imprisoning two cc's of air, and oh boy! now you're ready to light up at last. (This is the nerve-shattering scene). You strike a match, sneak stealthily in the direction of the lamp, twirl a thingamajig on the side of the doodad, and at the same time apply the match to the mantles. These look like tonsils, but they're the consistency of cobwebs—only much less durable—so of course they break when you point the match at them. Now you hunt for more mantles. When they are at last attached, you start on the sneaking-up bit again. This time the mantles catch with a roar like a cannon, and the flames leap six feet into the air. After three minutes of this fireworks display, the hateful thing finally settles down—and you have a light! The stench of the thing gives you a headache that lasts until morning; it hisses constantly, driving you one step nearer to a nervous breakdown; the light wobbles up   up

                  down   down

like a snake in the process of being charmed. But—well—it *is* a light. Of sorts. All this while 500,000,000,000,000 watts sizzle like crazy over the power line just two hundred yards away!

MONDAY, SEPTEMBER 23

Tonight must be Christmas—or my golden jubilee—or something! Tonight I had two visitors! They were Peg Barclay and Gertie Milne, who are teaching over at Ootischenia. I was in a tizzy of indecision as to whether to open the door in answer to their knock, or to pretend that I was a deaf mute, but the rap was followed by two voices carolling, "Open up, comrade!" Since they were unmistakably feminine, and undeniably pure Canadian, untainted by Doukhobor dialect, I unlocked my trusty Yale at once.

It was a lovely evening, such as I had forgotten existed except on weekends. They apologized for not coming sooner, but had been just as harried as I, and in comparing notes, we discovered that Ootischenia (translated—"Paradise"!) pupils and circumstances differ not one whit from those of Pleasant. They have invited me over for supper tomorrow night, and even if it does mean one whole evening minus the company of Hectograph, I shall certainly attend. If it should mean sliding on my posterior through dust all the way, I shall be there. If it meant slashing my way through ten thousand nude Sons of Freedom, I should be there. Ah, company! What bliss!

WEDNESDAY, SEPTEMBER 25

I skittered and scurried to get my work done after school yesterday, and headed for Ootischenia at 5.30. It was a pleasant, though dusty, walk through a shortcut which leads through the orchards suddenly reappearing half a mile or so beyond Pleasant. Beshawled women were out by the score harvesting apples, and shouting and laughing as they worked. They called greetings as I passed, and stared at me quite frankly. They are a gay, boisterous lot in the orchards, quite unlike the solid, sombre women of the big kitchens.

A little farther on I passed a cement foundation, all that is left of a former school which had been the target, at some time in the past, of incendiarism. From its skeleton, I could see that it had been identical with Pleasant, and I wondered how long it would be before Pleasant, too, would be levelled. There are nearly six hundred fanatics now in exile on Piers

Island, just off Vancouver Island, but are they *all* there? — I hope.

Peg and Gertie live in the big front room of the Makaoff house. Their furnishings are exactly like mine, except that they have a dozen or so orange crates serving as storage cupboards, shoe-closets, vegetable bins, wash-stands, end-tables, and bookcases. I'm sure the Sunkist people would be gratified to see such concentrated advertising on their behalf —and it doesn't cost them a penny!

We had just sat down to supper when a knock came at the door leading into the Makaoff kitchen. At the sound, my hostesses sprang into action—Peg grabbed the chop platter from the table and sent it skimming under her bed, while Gertie feverishly sprinkled dry coffee on top of the stove. (Elementary, my dear Watson: burning coffee blots out the odor of meat, and what is lurking under beds cannot be seen! The Doukhobors do not eat meat, ergo their teachers must not). Peg went to the door and opened it to admit Mrs. Makaoff laden with a huge bowl of borsch, and beaming broadly as she tendered it. When she left, the meat reappeared, and we sat down again. Actually the borsch, made with a great deal of butter in place of meat-stock, and containing every available vegetable—but with beets, of course, predominant—was quite delicious. But I swallowed each mouthful with the memory of Stoopnikoff's zooming flies outdoing the flavor of the soup, so I cannot truthfully say that I enjoyed it. Sometimes I think it would have been easier for me, and pleasanter, if I had not been brought up in a home where a stray fly was pursued relentlessly until put to death, for now I find myself involuntarily questioning the standards of cleanliness of anyone—some of them very nice people, too!—who will permit a fly to sail around unmolested. (Which reminds me that when I thought, the other day, to start an anti-fly campaign amongst my pupils, it only resulted in a fierce argument as to whose kitchen boasted the greatest number of the filthy little beasts.)

When the dishes were done, Peg and Gertie took me on a tour of inspection of their schoolrooms in, of all places, a (slightly) remodelled barn, so decrepit that I feared it would fall over under the pressure of a passing breeze. The doors squ-e-a-k like those in radio mystery dramas, and the floors are minus boards here and there. The rooms are beyond beautification, and yet the girls have made them almost cosy with bright pictures and crepe-paper curtains.

My new-found kindred spirits suggested that I remain overnight with them, and I needed no second invitation. It was pure, unadulterated bliss to be away from that lonely den of mine for an evening, and the thought of going to bed to *sleep* — instead of to listen, and to hold my breath for moments on end, and to tremble—was so exhilarating that I lay awake for hours savoring the delight of it. Long after the gas lamp had been put out of its hissing misery, I heard a faint spatter-trickle-spatter in the leaves of the grape vine outside the open window.

"Sounds like rain," I said sleepily.

Peg mumbled, " 'S not rain. 'S Paul — or maybe Sam." Mystified, I asked, "What do you mean, 'it's Paul or Sam'?"

"Well," she elucidated, "Mrs. Makaoff has a couple of visitors this week. And they're sleeping upstairs. And they don't care to go outside in the middle of the night. So — 's Paul. Or Sam. G' night."

? ? ? . . . OH . . . ! ! !

OCTOBER

TUESDAY, OCTOBER 1

HAVE visited several of my pupils' homes this past week and have found them all identical, even to the numbers of flies. I have occasionally heard that the Doukhobor homes are of the spotless you-can-eat-off-the-floor variety. So far I cannot add my testimonial to that report, but perhaps I have chosen the wrong homes to visit. In every village, however, hospitality to me is the keynote, and it must be an honor to have the teacher call, for on more than one occasion I have overheard a child say loftily, "And yesterday night teacher was at our plyace." This announcement invariably leads to a request from someone else, "And Meess Hulls, today you weell cawme my plyace?"

Peter Koochin asked me this afternoon if I would go home with him and look at his little brother's finger. He had chopped it with an axe a week ago, Peter said, and it was not healing very well. The Koochin village is less than a mile from the school so we were there by four o'clock. The mother gave me the same shy, but genuine, welcome that I have received everywhere I have called, and then took me into their "house" to see young Nick. His index finger on the left hand was bundled clumsily in a piece of navy-and-white cotton, anything but clean, which, when unrolled, revealed an ugly wound. The end of the finger was all but severed, and it had gathered and festered. As I thought

27

about blood poisoning, I stormed inwardly at the stupidity of anyone who would allow a thing like that to go unattended by a doctor and suggested to Peter, who interpreted for his mother, that he should tell her how serious this might be. When he had repeated this to her, and she had replied, Peter said, "And mawder say *you* can fyix like doctor, Meess Hulls, and she say for you to fyix."

I asked Peter if they had any kind of disinfectant. After a lengthy explanation of the meaning of "disinfectant", he finally said yes. This cheered me a bit — until he came back with a bottle of something black and syrupy called PAIN-KILLER. So back I went to the school for Lysol, bandages, and adhesive tape. After cleaning the finger, and applying a proper dressing, I explained to Mrs. Koochin that it was very unwise to put colored bandages on such a wound. She was most surprised to hear of such a strange thing, thanked me, and asked if I would come again to see how Nick was. She gave me a large bag of apples, but I have learned, to my great disappointment, that Brilliant apples are not my dish. The orchards here are infested with coddling moth, and every time you plunge your teeth into an apple, a fat, juicy worm rears his ugly head up into the great outdoors, wavers back and forth on his end, leers at you, and dares you to take another bite.

WEDNESDAY, OCTOBER 2

A week has gone by since my first meeting with Gertie and Peg, but it has been a very different week from those which preceded it. They had supper over here one night, and we have visited one or two evenings. It makes such a difference to have company, and I feel that I don't really mind Pleasant so much now — in the daytime. After-dark hours are still not my favorite time of day, and the slightest sound turns me hot and cold and lukewarm, all at once.

FRIDAY, OCTOBER 4

Had my first visit from the inspector today. I had antici-pated a severe attack of palsy at his appearance, but he was so friendly and helpful that I forgot all about shaking. He voiced his sympathy with me in the case of Tena Rezansoff, my five-year-old. Tena lolls in her seat, falls out of it a dozen times a day, and is eternally grovelling about on the floor in search of the things she drops every three minutes. She is a most untidy child whose clothes and face are always grubby and sticky. I was horrified, on the first day of school, to see flies strolling about on her face breakfasting, no doubt, on smears of jam from Tena's morning meal. She was not visibly annoyed by them but, out of habit, I guess, she would flick her tongue out to shoo them off. Tena's first assignment, every morning since then, has been to wash her face and hands. My other beginners are now able to understand simple instructions, and can even read a bit, but Tena absorbs nothing but her crayons and plasticine, which she devours avidly.

SUNDAY, OCTOBER 6

Peg, Gertie, and I all came out together on the bus tonight. They came in for coffee, but left at nine o'clock since they, too, have work to prepare for tomorrow. They had been gone only about five minutes when I heard someone on my doorstep. Thinking that they had forgotten something, I opened the door to find quite a personable looking young Doukhobor standing on the porch. He introduced himself very politely, and in good English, as Mike Fofanoff, and said that if I would allow him to do so, he would like to visit with me. I was undecided for a moment, but realized that it would not do to appear unfriendly, and since he seemed not at all bold, I said that he might come in for just a little while. He is a pleasant-appearing chap of perhaps eighteen or nineteen, and looks surprisingly well scrubbed. He turned out to be even not-*too*-bad company, for he talked fairly intelligently about a number of things. He thanked me for letting him come in and voluntarily departed at the end of fifteen or twenty minutes, asking whether I would mind if he came again. I told him that I was usually busy with school work and let it go at that.

MONDAY, OCTOBER 7

Have been over to look at Nick's finger again; it is still a horrible mess, and I wish that he could see a doctor. But my suggestion to that effect met with no enthusiasm whatever; it's unnecessary, and it would be expensive — "even might it would cost two or t'ree dollars yet" — so . . .

Today at recess, several of my pupils came rushing excitedly into the schoolroom, all exclaiming in turn, "And Meess Hulls, Neecky Stoochnoff ees een da toilet!"

Seeing nothing extraordinary in this event, I said casually, "Well, I suppose he'll come out when he's ready," and went on checking books.

"But you know, Meess Hulls, and Neecky ees een da toilet," repeated one of the informers.

The others shrieked, "And yes! And he ees een da toilet!"

"Oh, run out and play, all of you. Nicky will be out in a minute," I said, thinking that perhaps the indispensable Nicky was being impatiently awaited for his role in some game or other. In the next moment, however, this calm supposition was put to rout, for one of the excited children said, in tones of utmost urgency, "Oh, but Meess Hulls, and you don't know — Neecky ees EEN da toilet! He ees EEN! And he dossn't cawmes out. Neecky *cyan't* cawme out!

Fuming inwardly at this interruption, I strode out to remove the barrier from the door, or whatever else it was that was keeping Nicky a prisoner. Groups of children stood around the privy hooting and guffawing, and I was prepared to scold them for tormenting the diminutive Nicky. The door was not caught in any way, and I peered in to witness a most unusual sight: there was Nicky — but not *all* of him! Only his head and arms were in evidence and these stuck up out of one of the two holes. He hung there quite impassively, looking neither perturbed nor amused, neither uncomfortable nor embarrassed. Nicky is far above average in his school work but always dead-pan, never showing the slightest pleasure in my praise, as do others of my pupils. Even in this predicament, he was as unconcerned as though

he always spent an hour out of every day in this fashion. I gasped and squeaked, "Nicky! In the name of heaven, how did you get in there?"

He rolled his blue eyes up at me, blinked, and never changing his expression, he recited, "And I am playing wid da football and I am pooting da football on da hole and I am standing on da football to see eef eet weell hold and it dossn't holds." (A very ordinary explanation of a most commonplace occurrence, he implied).

I fished him out (leaving da football in its last resting place, needless to say), pointed him in the direction of his village, and said, "Go home, Nicky. Quickly!"

Even after taking a casual glance at his shoes, he showed no emotion of any kind, but set off at an everyday pace across the field. Nicky, I concluded, is a true stoic.

TUESDAY, OCTOBER 8

Mike Fofanoff called again this evening, bringing this time his guitar in order that he might "treat" me, he said, to some music. I am truly fond of music, but not of the guitar, especially one which has obviously seen its best days, and especially one which is played by a novice. And when the repertoire comprises Red Wing, Home on the Range, Swiss Chalet, Birmingham Jail, Red Wing, Show Me the Way to Go Home, Red Wing, Swiss Chalet, and Birmingham Jail, I am no longer sure that I like music — of *any* kind. But I suppose Mike's intentions were good, and it definitely was a change. However, this "treat" meant that I couldn't get at my work, so it will be later than ever now before I'm finished. Ho hum.

The wailing out on the road is at an all-time high tonight.

THURSDAY, OCTOBER 10

Polly Gevatkoff stayed after school today to do some corrections and her sister, Marion, waited for her. As Polly worked, Marion leaned over her shoulder watching. Suddenly Marion bellowed, "JESUS CHRIST, Polly! How you write!"

"Marion!" I cried. "What did you say?"

"And I say to Polly Jesus Christ how she write. And here's awful writing, Meess Hulls. You just lookit how awful!"

SUNDAY, OCTOBER 13

Peg and Gertie have just left after a reviving cup of coffee. We had such loads of groceries tonight that the last mile seemed like ten. A three-mile jaunt on a brisk fall evening is anybody's meat, but oh, this trek every Sunday night with a week's provisions! We pack everything, literally, from soup to nuts.

Had just settled down to work when there was a knock at the door. I was sure it would be Mike again, and was not too pleased at another interruption so soon after his last visit. It was not Mike, but one of his compatriots — John Markin this time. His instrument was a mandolin, and his programme was made up the following: Show Me the Way to Go Home, Red Wing, Swiss Chalet, Home on the Range, Red Wing, Swiss Chalet, Birmingham Jail, and Red Wing. John's Birmingham Jail has nine more verses than Mike's version. Oh yes, they *sing*, too!

When not playing, John rolls innumerable lumpy cigarettes from an evil-smelling tobacco, and uses those horrible yellow papers which get all juicy. Since both musical instruments and smoking are forbidden fruits amongst the Doukhobors, my place will probably become a hideout for all sinful young stuff. Drinking and dancing are also high on the list of the devil's works, but Allah be praised, I have seen no evidence of drinking, and my rooms aren't spacious enough for dancing.

John left at ten o'clock to join the banshees on the road, no doubt, and when I crept into bed at 12.30, the eerie howls were still resounding through the inky blackness. Sometimes I wish it would rain buckets every night of the week (except Friday); a downpour seems to be the only thing which discourages coyote-howl practice!

33

MONDAY, OCTOBER 14

Nick's finger is definitely on the mend at last, so I don't think I need to continue my trips to the Koochin village. On my way back from there tonight, I called in at the Abrossimoff village. Mrs. Abrossimoff is positively the hugest structure this side of the Taj Mahal. Her assorted stomachs and breasts and chins are piled tier on tier in the most fascinating arrangement, and each vies with the others to be the jigglingest. Her skin is tanned to a deep, leathery brown, her cheeks are like Jonathan apples, and her eyes are dark and glowing. She, like all the others, took me to see her "house" and the newest little Abrossimoff, who lay in his suspended cradle. He was rolled round and round in a blanket, arms pinned down inside it, so that the only movable part of him was his head. Despite the fact that he was indoors — and apparently has always been there, judging from his grey-plasticine complexion — he wore a bonnet tied securely under his chin. In his mouth was a "pacifier", made from a piece of rag, knotted, and dipped in a solution of sugar and water — a most appetizing looking morsel! Whenever he spat it out, which he did every seven seconds, (and who wouldn't?) his fond mother immediately jammed it into his reluctant mouth again, and Michael and Pauline explained that "all babies like dis shoogar ryag vyery moch." What with blankets, bonnets, heat, and "shoogar ryags", I don't know how these babies survive at all, poor little mites. This one's older brother and sister admire him without reservation, and Michael said lovingly, "And, Meess Hulls, eesn't he cyute leetle bawger?"

The Abrossimoffs want this baby's birth registered, and have asked me to see to it in Nelson this weekend. This request was a great surprise to me, since Doukhobors generally will have nothing to do with the registration of births, deaths, nor marriages. Their refusal to comply with government regulations in this respect had its origin in Russia centuries ago. At that time, the Doukhobors departed from the Greek Orthodox Church, which handled the registrations; and in leaving the Church, they also abandoned the practice of registration. But perhaps the Abrossimoffs'

desire to register this baby's birth will mark the beginning
of a gradual acceptance of Canadian laws; or maybe it is
only that this one family is a bit more progressive than
the others. At any rate, registered little Alec shall be. I
left with a sugar bag full of tomatoes, apples — and PLUMS.

WEDNESDAY, OCTOBER 16

Had supper with Peg and Gertie tonight. When I entered their abode, I wondered what calamity had overtaken
the place. The curtains were all down, the table was laid
with newspaper, and each place was set with a tin plate and
an empty coffee can for a cup. The girls were barefooted,
and dressed in rags.

"Hard times supper," said Peg, as she placed a huge pot
of beans in the centre of the table. Not any of your savory
baked beans, with their tantalizing aroma of molasses, mus-
tard, salt pork, and onions. These were just BEANS—plain
. . . boiled . . . beans — great big brown fellows. There was
no choice but to eat them, for there was nothing else anywhere in sight, except the cans filled with black coffee. For
a few moments I felt that at any second they would stop the
nonsense and produce at least a pot of cheap stew; but no,
this was in dead earnest. When I felt that I could never
be civil to another bean as long as I might live, Peg offered
Gertie and me each fifty cents to finish the horrible things.
Gertie, who is of Scottish descent, accepted the challenge;
that was not surprising. But so did I — I, who sprang from
the loins of the Vikings and have not, to my knowledge, a
single Scottish ancestor in my pedigree.

The misery we suffered bears no description. But Peg
had a wonderful time. And Gertie and I each have fifty
cents.

FRIDAY, OCTOBER 18

Slept over at the beanery on Wednesday night, so was all
freshened up for last night's visit from *both* Mike and
John. Mike had a ukulele, and John a mouth organ. Their
programme embraced the same delightful numbers as previously, with All My Sins Are Taken Away thrown in as

an extra. They asked whether they might leave their instruments here, since they worry that they might be found at home. Foreseeing a nightmarish future in this arrangement, I refused permission, saying that my quarters are too small to accommodate anything more than they already contain.

They were both conversationally inclined tonight, and agreed that they are not going to always live in the community. Nor are they going to marry Doukhobor girls. Said John, "The old people don't want us to leave the community, but me, I don't care what they say, I am going to go out and work. If I had better education, I could get a real good job and build my own house someplace. The old people say, 'What use is school? Why you need school to plow land?' As soon as the law lets, they make us not go to school any more. They are all crazy!"

Mike's question caught me unawares. "How much do you get a month for teaching school, Miss Hulls?"

"Oh," I replied, after a moment's hesitation, "just about enough to pay my expenses, Mike."

"Sure! You have education. You are lucky. I bet you get thirty, or maybe even *forty* dollars a month! If I had been let to school after I was fifteen, I bet I could earn like that, too!"

I suppose if any of them knew that my salary exceeds even the enormous sum of forty dollars, the old people would raise a loud hue and cry, and might even go so far as to "tyell gawverment."

This threat of tyelling gawverment always arises in any altercation. Gawverment, I surmise, is a mighty being— superhuman, or otherwise — who sits in state somewhere, possibly Victoria, although I have never heard this as fact! —and who is a most terrible and awe-inspiring monster. At any rate, the mention of this mysterious and all-powerful character usually has a more or less quieting effect in a squabble; even the children use the threat to strike fear into the hearts of their adversaries.

MONDAY, OCTOBER 21

Mrs. Abrossimoff, Michael, and Pauline were here at 7.30 this morning, to see whether I had registered the baby. They brought me some plums! They were all very pleased that this momentous event had taken place, but little did they know with what embarrassment to me!

I entered the Court House on Saturday morning, marched up to the desk, and announced that I wished to register a birth. At the time, I could see nothing extraordinary about my remarks to the clerk, and it was only when I gave her the last necessary information regarding the baby that I realized what sort of impression I must have given her. When I made my announcement, she looked a trifle startled — I recalled that *later*—for although we do not know one another personally, each of us knows the other's name. But she reached for the forms and, all business, asked briskly, "Name of child?"

"Alec Abrossimoff," I answered pleasantly. She winced —I recalled that later, too.

"Father?"

"John Abrossimoff," I said smiling. She looked disgusted.

"Residence?"

"Brilliant."

"And . . . ah . . . er . . . you are the . . . er . . . mother?" she queried from the length of her ten-foot pole.

"Who, ME?" I squawked, as I finally began to wake up. "Oh, my gosh! Oh, for heaven's sake, NO! I'm only registering this birth for the baby of one of my fathers — I mean, for the pupil of one of my babies — that is, for the babies of one of my parents — look, I only *teach* out there!"

Anyway, little Alec Abrossimoff has a birth certificate. And if it should ever be lost, I can certainly testify to the fact that his birth was definitely registered.

As well as being the day upon which Alec A. received his precious document, it is also my birthday, so I asked Gertie and Peg over for supper by way of celebration. They didn't know that it was an "occasion", but they surely came attired for one. When I opened the door, there they stood, decked out in evening dresses, dripping with necklaces, bracelets, and earrings, plastered with makeup, and oozing perfume. Two more likely-looking madames I have never seen. They said they had just felt like dressing up, and thought they might as well do it up brown. They would have stayed the night with me, but could scarcely be seen traipsing home in those outfits at eight in the morning.

We have decided that, instead of carting all our provisions out from Nelson, we will go to Castlegar once a week and buy our groceries at the two or three small stores there. It will lessen our weekend load, give us a break in the week, and have disastrous effects (we hope) on our waistlines, since it is between five and six miles to that centre.

It will also eliminate one evening of Doukhobor visitors each week; Peg and Gertie are having the same round of entertainment as I, and they don't relish it any more than I do.

My "mailmen" brought me several interesting parcels from the post office after school, making the day truly birthdayish.

These children do not conform with any others I know. They coax to go for my mail, which means a hike of six miles all told; they squabble amongst themselves for the privilege (?) of washing my dishes, and even of scrubbing my floors; they haggle over who shall chop my kindling, and who shall peel my vegetables. They are altogether revolutionary to my previous concept of youngsters, who have seemed to me to be forever inventing ways of getting *out* of doing chores. I do not pay them for these jobs, for I think that might lead to serious complications; but I give them oranges or cookies sometimes, or a bit of pretty ribbon, or some tiny trinket. Often I have not a thing with which to repay them, but they are still just as eager to help me the next time. In addition to these voluntary tasks, they take turns doing the entire janitor work in the schoolroom, for which they receive no remuneration whatever from the Department of Education.

TUESDAY, OCTOBER 22

Tonight, I had no less than *six* young men come a-calling. I fear that Mike and John have paved the way for the more timorous swains and I am now to be deluged with visitors practically every evening. I appreciate friendly overtures — in moderation — but cannot have this steady stream of company night after night. My lost hours of work are not even compensated for by lively conversation, nor even interesting chatter, for all attempts at discussion, except in the cases of Mike and John, are left entirely to me. Their only contributions are "yes", "no", and "hee-hee". In roughly three and a half minutes, I have asked them everything which can be answered by yes, no, and hee-hee; and there I am, stranded in a pool of deep silence. So from here on, I shall go on with my work, and if they take any pleasure from just sitting, they may sit and sit.

THURSDAY, OCTOBER 24

This afternoon we are off to the Teachers' Convention to be held in Trail tomorrow and Saturday.

SUNDAY, OCTOBER 27

We're mad! We watched City Teachers performing in their gilded cages. We saw those paragons standing on their oiled floors, under electric lights, surrounded by pianos, metronomes, maps, globes, typewriters, mimeograph machines, and miles of blackboards — teaching *one grade each*.

And dot's not fyair. And we're gonna tyell gawverment!

MONDAY, OCTOBER 28

Regularity of attendance leaves much to be desired in all Doukhobor schools. Bill Harasimoff was absent this morning, and at noon I asked for his reason. Written excuses are not demanded here, as in other schools, since so many of the parents are unable to write English. Bill didn't look at me as he answered, "And I was hyelping fawder-my."

Usually the reply is, "And I hyad to carry da cow to da pyasture," or "And I hyad to go meeting." (These meetings go on and on, and I have never been able to learn their purpose, nor their outcome, nor why even the children are compelled by their parents to go). Since Bill's answer appeared to be evasive, I went on, "What were you doing?"

He repeated, "And Meess Hulls, I was helping fawder-my."

I should have known better than to insist, but by now I was determined to have a valid excuse for his absence, so quite firmly I asked again just *how* he had helped his father. Served me right, I guess, when he blurted, "And da cow was getting a calf, and da calf dossn't cawmes, and fawder-my was tying a rope on da calf's hyead, and he was tyelling me to pooll, and I was poolling."

TUESDAY, OCTOBER 29

Last night I was awakened by the most terrific crash against the north wall of the schoolroom. It seemed as though something huge had been dashed against the building with great force; but it was not followed by the slightest other sound. The night literally throbbed with silence — and I with fear. I was too nervous to move enough to reach for my flashlight to look at the time, but it must have been well on into the small hours, for even the nocturnal singers were not abroad. For the first time, I wished that there were a thousand of them chanting right under my window. I looked this morning to see whether I could find any clue as to what it could have been, but there was no sign of any person, or thing, having been near the building.

Oh dear, just when I'm beginning to get a little (very little!) braver, something like this has to set me all a-jangle again.

Not a single pupil turned up at either school this morning. Peg and Gertie came over, and we decided to follow the hordes of people who had been trailing down the road to Brilliant since early morning. This is the anniversary of the death of Peter "Lordly" Veregin, original leader of

40

the Doukhobors, who was killed on this date in 1924 in the mysterious bombing of a C.P.R. passenger coach at Farran, fifty-eight miles west of Nelson.

When we arrived at the station, we found hundreds of Doukhobors gathered there, all attired in their best finery. Many had come from other points in the province to attend this annual memorial service for the dead leader. Soon they formed into a long procession, and began the slow ascent up the steep hillside to the site of Peter Lordly's tomb. The shrine is a white marble edifice, erected on an elevated, beautifully-kept rectangle of green lawn, directly above the turbulent Kootenay River. There are trees and flowers bordering the plot, and the whole is enclosed by a fence of narrow iron railing. It is the one spot in the entire community where any attempt has been made at beautification and, due to the constant loving care which it receives, is truly lovely.

When all the mourners had arrived, they stood in solid crowds outside the fence, women to one side and men to the other, and paid silent tribute to the memory of the man who had been their Christ. Then they raised their voices in a plaintive, mournful chant, somehow beautiful there on the stony hillside, in spite of its raucous quality, and as they sang, many a face was wet with tears.

A ceremony followed in which representative members of the group walked around the crypt, and offered prayers before the white monument with its carved doves and wheat sheaves. This ritual of singing and praying continued for two hours or more, and between the hymns and prayers the members bowed deeply to one another before a table upon which had been placed the bread, salt, and water symbolical of the spirit of Christ, hospitality, and the grace of God, respectively.

This congregation was not the size of the one which gathered for Peter's funeral in 1924. The newspaper reports of that service gave the number of mourners as twenty thousand. They came from all Doukhobor communities in Canada, and the entire surrounding hillsides were filled with worshippers. But the spirit of today's gathering was the same — one of deep reverence and love for the leader who had come with them from Russia.

Their love and trust has not rested on Peter Lordly's son, Peter Petrovich, who arrived from Russia three years after his father's death. He is now their acknowledged leader, but under him the Union of Spiritual Communities of Christ in its true conception of ideals appears to be fast disintegrating. Peter the Purger, as he calls himself, is of the "do-as-I-say, not-as-I-do" school, and disgusts his people with his roustabout drinking orgies, gambling sessions, and general debauchery. Peg, Gertie, and I have more than once seen him on Trail streets, disgustingly intoxicated, and shouting obscenities of the vilest kind. Despite their contempt of him, still the people are under his thumb and continue, unwillingly according to Mike and John who have spoken of this to me, to raise money to support him in his evil ways.

He is a coarse, repulsive-looking man not yet forty years of age, but appearing much older, due undoubtedly to his constant dissipation. His complexion is pasty-white, in contrast to his very dark hair and moustache. In morals, ideals, and appearance, he is the antithesis of his father, Peter Lordly, whom I remember seeing in my childhood and whom I recall as a rather impressive-looking man with a snow-white goatee. Certainly this renegade son of his would make him bow his head in shame were he here to see all that goes on.

When the mourners had all made their way back down the hillside and had left only a handful of the head figures of the ceremony standing around the tomb, we went over to ask permission to take one or two pictures of the edifice. This request they willingly granted, but when I stood before it and was ready to snap the shutter of my camera, great consternation arose. The sun behind me cast my shadow on the face of the monument and this, they said, could not be allowed. Therefore I had to take my picture from farther back, where the shadow would not be imposed upon the shrine.

Since it was still early, we went over to Castlegar to do some shopping. We were able to find everything we wanted at the three general stores there. The proprietor of one of them, Mr. Duchak, seems most genial, and was filled with pity for us at the thought that we had walked all that way. He is a very chipper little man with sparkling blue eyes, white hair, and a dazzling smile. He lives with his daughter Elsa, who helps him in the store and keeps house for him. He introduced us to her, almost apologetically we thought— and no wonder! She is as sour and gloomy as her sprightly father is sweet and cheerful. She obviously disapproved of us, our high spirits, and our slacks, and acknowledged the introductions with a bored, painful "H'ja do."

Elsa is about thirty, the most drab, unsparkling thirty I have ever seen; her shoulders slump dejectedly, and she sags in the middle. She wears her black hair in a complex arrangement of dips and frizzes which extend across her forehead, almost shading her disinterested grey eyes. I find it very difficult to believe that this miserable lump was sired by jovial little Mr. Duchak, but perhaps Elsa's mother was a Gorgon who had stronger genes than her husband.

Rubbing his hands together, Mr. Duchak said heartily —and to our delight — "Well now, you young ladies could do with a cup of tea before you start back on that long walk. Elsa, make us all some tea, will you, and maybe some of that chocolate cake you made this morning would be the very right thing about now! Come along into the kitchen, young ladies."

We were so eager to get at the tea and the cake, that we all but trod on the heels of the reluctant Elsa, who favored her poor unfortunate father with a dark frown of disapproval for his lovely, lovely suggestion. A customer entered the store just then, so Mr. Duchak waited to serve him, while Elsa jabbed chairs at us, and said graciously, "I *suppose* you'd better take off your jackets. It's kind of warm in here."

With Elsa around, there was nothing warm about the place, but we thanked her and happily removed the jackets. And waited for her to make with the tea. And the chocolate cake. It turned out to be the most unElsalike cake in the world. It was THIS high, and absolutely bee-yoo-ti-ful ! —

43

and we drooled copiously while we watched her cut five pieces and transfer them to plates. As her father entered from the store, she said, "I suppose you *all* take *both* cream and sugar?"

Simultaneously, Peg said, "No sugar, please," and Gertie said, "No cream, thank you." In my desire not to displease Elsa too much before I had my piece of cake securely anchored down with my fork, I said nothing, so my tea, when she passed it to me, was clear. Peg gushed, not without reason, "What delicious cake, Miss Duchak!"

Gertie and I said, truthfully, m'm'm and isn't it? and wonderful!

"Huh," acknowledged Elsa graciously.

Mr. Duchak wiped his mouth and said, "Indeed it is. Elsa is a pretty good cook."

"Perhaps you'll give us the recipe sometime?" quavered Gertie.

"Just an ordinary chocolate cake recipe," grunted Elsa, conveying the impression that any dolt could turn out a masterpiece like this, and that her recipe would go with her to the grave. She didn't offer us a second piece, but it didn't matter because none of us would have dared to accept another anyway.

We asked Mr. Duchak whether he knew of anyone who could supply us with fresh eggs. Not many of the Doukhobors keep chickens, and those who do have sufficient eggs for no more than their own use. He said that we might be able to obtain them from the postmaster at Brilliant, Mr. Lipinski.

We didn't tarry long after we had finished our tea, for we felt too sorry for poor little Mr. Duchak who tried so hard, and so in vain, to thaw out the long icicle he has for a daughter.

As we were leaving, he caroled, "Be sure to come in whenever you are over this way. The kettle is always boiling, you know."

(A sound like "hyrmph" or "snf" came from Elsa's direction).

I don't think that business is Mr. Duchak's only motive; I feel that he is just naturally given to the spirit of good fellowship, and truly likes people. Elsa, for the first time, showed some enthusiasm when she sighed loudly, and groaned, "G'*bye*."

We went in to Lipinski's on the way home. Of course we had seen Mr. L. several times when calling for our mail, but we had never visited, nor had we met his wife.

They are Polish, I think, and we found them most friendly and pleasant. Mr. Lipinski is a huge boxcar of a man whose chin spills over his collar onto his barrel chest which overflows onto his enormous stomach which threatens to some day obscure his lap. His eyes and hair are black as tar, and he sports a widespread, ferocious looking moustache. He booms good-naturedly at everything and everyone, including his string-bean wife, who is as fair as he is dark, and as gaunt as he is voluminous. They said that they could supply us with fresh eggs, and also with freshly churned butter if we wish, so that is one more thorn out of our co-operative side. It would seem, these days, that everything is coming up roses!

WEDNESDAY, OCTOBER 30

Mary Zoobkoff came over after school to ask me if I would get her mother a glass pitcher in town this weekend — "peenk, if you could find like dot." I have done several bits of shopping for various people, since there are no cars out here and as a result few of my neighbors ever leave Brilliant. Hope the pitcher won't take up too much room in my bag.

THURSDAY, OCTOBER 31

I gave my pupils a Hallowe'en party this afternoon. They had contrived costumes of various inconsistencies, and I gave each a mask. It was bedlam, and they had a wonderful time, in the universal way of children at parties everywhere — more wonderful, perhaps, since a party is a rare occasion in their lives. Halfway through the festivities, I had them march around the room and as they passed me, I distributed bags, each containing an assortment of candies and a balloon. Nicky Stoochnoff (he of the football which dossn't holds) peered into his bag and mumbled, "Byetter eef eet would be fire-cryackers."

I wonder . . . the bomb influence? ? ?

NOVEMBER

SUNDAY, NOVEMBER 3

BROUGHT Mrs. Zoobkoff's pitcher, a shoddy Woolworth affair — in bright pink glass — certain, I knew, to please. Mary was here, waiting impatiently for me to arrive with it. There were three or four others with her, and when she unwrapped it, they all went into ecstasies, squealing, "E-h-h, and lookit how preety!"

"Polly! Myary! Lookit how ni-ice!"

"Eh-h-h, Meess Hulls, and where you bought so lawvely jawg?"

"E-h-h, how preety eet ees !"

"And how moch dos eet cost like dis jawg?"

Mary was the envy of all, and that query about the cost of the pitcher presages no good for me, I am almost certain. I'll probably be a weekly jug-lugger from now on, until every family has just one like it, and is thus able to hold up its head before the Zoobkoffs.

MONDAY, NOVEMBER 4

Peg and Gertie came over after school to inform me that their place had been broken into while they were in town, but that nothing had been stolen except a jar in which they had been putting all their pennies, and which contained something between two and three hundred of them.

47

They also related a story which proves the matchless hospitality of the Doukhobors. Someone had belatedly taken the spirit of Hallowe'en to heart, and hauled away their little grey house sometime during the week-end. But one of their neighbors had come to the rescue, gallantly offering, "And no myatter, you can use our shyithouse. Go ahyead!"

We have all been kindly invited by several to use their bath-house facilities whenever we wish. Indoor plumbing of any kind—except for the cold-water galvanized sink—is unheard of. In fact, my pupils were astounded when one day, in casual conversation, I happened to mention a hot-water tap. They had never heard of such a wondrous thing as *hot* water from a *tap*—"eh-h-h! Meess Hulls, and how it gyets *hot*, da water?"

Each village has its own bath-house — a small building out back amongst the shed-barn-privy conglomeration. There are no tubs; Doukhobor ablutions are performed in a unique way of their own. Two or three benches are arranged on a platform in step fashion, and rocks of many sizes are piled on the floor. In preparation for a bath, you light a big fire in the stove, and fill the huge container on top of it with water. When the water is boiling, the next step is to pour it upon the icy rocks — presto! vast quantities of billowing steam. You sit, nude of course, on the bottom step, wallowing in the swirling steam until you are acclimatized to the heat. As it becomes bearable, you ascend step by step, to the top, where it becomes almost impossible to breathe — more boiling water being tossed on the rocks at intervals.

Well — it does open the pores! If that's what you were after — open, rather than closed, pores. One of the main drawbacks, however, is that sooner or later you have to *leave*. And as you dash for the house, all the frigid air — that's been hanging around outside, waiting for you — comes galloping at all those opened pores. What a SH-SHOCK!

TUESDAY, NOVEMBER 5

Regular visits from Mike and John are still the order of the day, or rather, of the night. Not only they, but scores of others haunt me, some with musical instruments, some without, but all equally boring. Sometimes they bring girl friends with them, and then it is even worse, for the girls twist and squirm and giggle and titter incessantly, with less reason — impossible as it may seem — than even the boys. But I am becoming more and more careless with the rules of etiquette, and now go on with my work regardless of their presence. Contrary to what *I* feel, they all believe that the hectograph pad is the most outstanding accomplishment in the world of science and, had they ever heard of Mr. Nobel, would unquestionably vote its fiendish perpetrator for one of his prizes.

There is one bright spot in these soirees — I am not expected to serve refreshments. At least, I don't *think* I am.

Since Sunday evening, I have had seven orders for "peenk jawgs like Mrs. Zoobkoff hyave." I wonder whether Mr. Woolworth would put me on commission?

WEDNESDAY, NOVEMBER 6

We went to Castlegar this evening, but did not see the scintillating Elsa. We concluded that she must have seen us first.

On the way back, we called in at Lipinski's for our eggs and butter. Mrs. L. insisted that we go in for tea, and after three solid hours in the cold air, we required very little in the way of persuasion. She led us proudly into her spotless little living room and we sat down amongst the world's (I am sure) most complete collection of house plants, doilies, antimacassars, vases, and photographs. These last were of Polish kin, whose relationship she painstakingly explained. But it was upon the last one that she poured forth most of her admiration.

"And this," she crooned fondly, "is our dear nephew, Joe, who will soon come to help Papa. He is now working on a farm in Alberta, but soon he will come. Joe we love like a son."

Joe's picture was then passed back and forth, and we congratulated Mrs. L. on her choice of nephews. His photo shows him to be a fat, cherubic-looking specimen of about thirty-five, with dimpled cheeks and blonde hair definitely on its way out. An anemic little moustache adorns his top lip, and he wears that other form of hirsute decoration that is even more obnoxious than a moustache — sideburns. We are so weary of sideburns; nearly all the swains out here cultivate the horrible things, the longer the handsomer, apparently.

Gertie asked, "Do you expect Joe very soon?" Not that she gave a darn.

"Oh my, yes," twittered Mrs. Lipinski joyfully, "he will be here in maybe two weeks now. Then you must come down often, for you will be good company for our dear Joe, and Joe you will all love, I am sure."

Joe's in for a heap o' lovin' looks as if!

THURSDAY, NOVEMBER 7

Went out to the shed for a stick of wood a few minutes ago, leaving the door ajar as usual. There's a wild wind blowing tonight, so of course the door blew shut. When I tried to get in, I found it locked — naturally — since I always leave the Yale lock on from inside. Nothing for it but to break a window, so now I can lie awake all night waiting for some nameless horror to bash in the cardboard which John, who arrived a moment later, fastened over the pane-less window.

FRIDAY, NOVEMBER 8—In Town

Now this is really an alluring spectacle! I should be in the fashion plates, there's no doubt about it.

When we left for the bus after school, the elements were doing themselves proud in whipping up the foulest wind-and rainstorm since the time of the Ark. Nothing on earth, short of death, would keep us from getting to town for weekends, however, so we tucked our heads down on our chests and proceeded to brave the fury of the weather. The time required to walk three miles allows one to soak up a stupendous amount of water when it is descending in solid sheets, so by the time we had reached the highway we were positively oozing moisture, clean through even our coats.

The bus was 'way late, and as we stood shivering, we noticed an old shack just below the road and decided to go into it for shelter. We found that it had only an earthen floor, so — why not light a fire and at least try to get warm? No sooner said than done, and we huddled around the meagre blaze and felt the same glow of wonder that the caveman must have experienced when he first discovered fire. But the caveman wore only his hairy chest and a deerhide diaper. He didn't prance around in a knee-length coat, with a crepe dress dangling a foot below it, as I did today. As my horrible dress dried slightly, all the pretty pebbly little things that cause material to be called "crepe", contracted and squeezed themselves up together until they occupied roughly about one-sixth of their original space. I backed away from the fire — but it was too late. The miserable process went on and on, and by the time the bus arrived, there was no dress visible at all — just my great, long legs below the coat. The other passengers were fascinated (I know this, because they giggled) by this amazing new style, and Peg and Gertie tried to pretend that I wasn't with them; but I kept talking to them, and poking them, and didn't let them get away with it. I think that most of the passengers concluded, finally, that those two would-be traitors were taking me in to the Welfare Office, or the Salvation Army, for a donation of clothing more adequate for the weather.

But by far the worst moment came when I had to get off the bus in town. It looked as though every person living in Nelson had come to meet that bus, and the depot was milling with people as I nonchalantly (?) made my way into the office to call a taxi. I prayed that I might wake up and find that it had been one of those frustrating dreams, but prayers are often not answered. This one was not.

SUNDAY, NOVEMBER 10

When we arrived back late this afternoon, several of my older pupils were waiting to tell me that "sawmeteeng fonny" had happened to Vera and Bill Katelnikoff's mother.

51

Mrs. Katelnikoff has always appeared sullen and morose, with none of the rumbling good nature of most of the Doukhobor women. Not so long ago she had a baby, and since then we have heard several stories about the "fonny" things she has done, and have suspected that all is not as it should be, mentally, with Mrs. K.

When one of the boys announced in hushed tones that she had this afternoon suddenly taken to running and singing through the wet, muddy fields, we knew that this was IT. Apparently no one had been able to catch her, or perhaps they were afraid to try, since she was brandishing a long butcher knife, but the last report had it that she had screeched that she was going to visit Pleasant scholnitsa (that's ME ! !) tonight.

Saying that heh-heh, it was nothing, and of course she wouldn't come here, heh-heh, I sent the youngsters home. We came in, made sure — four times — that the door was locked, (purely habit, of course), lit the fire, and proceeded to drink coffee. I don't know why they didn't run like gazelles, but the chalk-white Gertie, and the pearl-grey Peg offered to stay with pale green me "for awhile."

We sat for hours, talking about everything except Mrs. Katelnikoff, and thinking about nothing except Mrs. Katelnikoff. We made feeble attempts to eat, but somehow coffee had fewer lumps to stick in our throats.

"It's so d-d-dark and w-w-wet," gabbled Peg, "I think we m-m-might as well stay the night and g-g-go over in the morning."

"Oh, s-s-sure!" quavered Gertie. "It's raining too hard to s-slosh home now."

Relief surged over me in waves as I heard the words of these two kind, lovely, thoughtful, generous, wonderful, unselfish, *brave* idols, and I tried to think of some great sacrifice I could make in their behalf. I even forgave them for disowning me because of my queer attire last Friday night.

And so time went on, and on, with one or another of us suggesting at ten-minute intervals that we might as well go to bed, ho hum, and the other two agreeing heartily, yaw-w-wn, and all of us sitting there.

At last, we heard someone coming up the steps, and I grew all wiggly inside, and something in my head went BO-N-N-NG like in the Fu Manchu movies and Gertie and Peg each picked up a big stick of wood and I grabbed my butcher knife and prayed that it was longer and sharper than Mrs. Katelnikoff's and I poked it straight in front of me and I yanked the door open and there stood . . . JOHN!

"Oh-h-h-, Cohn! Jome in!" I groaned.

He looked a bit perplexed, did my lovely John, at being greeted by three females so well armed with such crude weapons, yet so obviously delighted to see him. We had it all explained to him in a few moments, and he put our minds (and knees) at rest, dear John, by telling us that they had caught Mrs. Katelnikoff and locked her up. Early in the evening, she had slithered into the well — to do her washing, she said — and it was there that several of the men had finally subdued her.

The well is a sort of reservoir, measuring roughly twenty-five feet square, for storing water for irrigation purposes. Luckily the water is not deep at this time of year, or poor Mrs. Katelnikoff might have been drowned.

We were so grateful to John for not being Mrs. K. that we put the pot on again, and plied him with coffee and sandwiches. When he had gone and Gertie, really meaning it this time, suggested bed, we all tumbled in and I wondered drowsily whether I would really have plunged my knife into Mrs. K., or have scrambled out between her legs and been loping up Nelson's Baker Street by now. Just as Peg nudged Gertie, and Gertie nudged me — the signal that Peg wished to turn over on her other side, so we would all have to do likewise — it occurred to me that maybe, just maybe, these two brave pals weren't so brave after all! In fact, it is possible that they were too darned *scared* to go home tonight! Thank goodness.

TUESDAY, NOVEMBER 12

Heard the end of a squabble between Johnny Perepelkin

and Alec Zarikoff today. Johnny fired the ultimate shot
of insult when he leered at Alec, "And fawder-your ees not
even on Piers Island, and fawder-my *ees* — yah!"

There are only a few children here whose parents are
in the Piers Island Penitentiary. These are billeted with
other families, and they wave their superiority over the
children of law-abiding Doukhobors like golden banners. A
Doukhobor apprehended as a Son of Freedom assumes the
role of a heroic martyr, gathers up his britches, and marches
proudly and triumphantly off to jail.

Nude parades reached an all-time high summer before
last when hundreds of Sons daily marched the highway
towards Nelson. This mass taking-off was their fanatical
protest at the fact that Peter Veregin had been jailed in
Saskatchewan for perjury. Several times they reached the
edge of town, and were the despair of the provincial and
city police. When two or three are bundled into the Black
Maria for disrobing, half a dozen others launch a protest
by also undressing, and they, in turn, are hustled in with
the first culprits. And since a Son sees no disgrace in going
to jail, it is only seconds before ten more jubilantly say, "Me
too", and unhitch their trousers or skirts. This burlesque
gathers momentum, and in a matter of minutes there are
empty clothes and raw Sons all over the place.

There is another class of people just as disgusting as
the Sons of Freedom in their antics. These are the righteous
citizens who, when word reaches town that a nude parade
is in progress fifteen or more miles out, drop whatever they
are doing, grab their cameras, pile excitedly into cars, and
drive like demons in order to get to Shoreacres, or Thrums,
or wherever the event is taking place, before it is all over.
Two hours later they are back, films all exposed, tsk-tsking
and clucking at the disgraceful, obscene, vile Doukhobors.
Before they go reluctantly home to salvage what is left of
the burnt roast, they dash to the photographer and tell him
to get those prints done as soon as possible . . . "Wait'll you
see these, Mac! They're really *something*, yes *sir!*" The
women, meantime, are waiting in the cars, licking their
chops and simpering, "My dear, aren't they just too, too

54

revolting?" and hoping there'll be another demonstration tomorrow.

WEDNESDAY, NOVEMBER 13

Sneaked into Duchak's store before Elsa knew we were there. Her father didn't seem to be around, so what could she do, poor thing, but wait on us. We all greeted her and Gertie said, "And how are you? We haven't seen you for awhile."

She drew her sagging shoulders up one-tenth of an inch, sighed deeply, and moaned, "Oh, I'm alright, I guess. I don't feel very good, but I'm not too bad."

None of us could decide, without consultation, whether this was good, or too bad, so without further queries we ordered our supplies, which Elsa wrapped with brown paper and more sighs and moans. Knowing that there was no hope of tea with Mr. Duchak not in evidence, we departed as soon as possible, leaving the frustrated (we think) Elsa staring disconsolately at her shelves of canned goods.

The moment Mrs. Lipinski opened the door, we knew that IT had come to pass. She was wreathed in wide smiles, and bubbling with unrestrained joy as she gave us the gladsome tidings in phrases than ran all over one another in their eagerness to be spoken.

"Oh, my dears, come in, come in! You can't know — oh, my goodness — a week early — you'll never guess! What do you suppose? — just tonight! Our Joe is here! Joe, Joe! Come and meet the girls, Joe!"

But before he could appear, Mrs. L. had pushed us all into the living-room, and there we were — in the Presence! Joe sat on the leather-upholstered throne that is the big old-fashioned rocking chair, flanked on one side by the gramophone, and on the other by his aunt's gangling rubber plant, whose tentacles, I swear, were reaching out caressingly towards Joe. He was puffing daintily at a cigar, but put it down at our appearance, and leaped to his feet with the suddenness of bread popping out of an automatic toaster. He was delighted, positively deeeeelighted to meet us, he said, and in shaking hands (we found out when we compared notes later) gave each a special sort of clammy little squeeze at the conclusion of the pumping — a sort of *you-are-the-babe-for-me-kiddo* squeeze.

Mrs. Lipinski hovered and fluttered about him like a butterfly over a flower, which is precisely what Joe is to her. She placed a footstool for him, emptied his ashtray, trotted to the kitchen for matches, patted his arm, and twittered unceasingly. Mr. Lipinski came charging in from the barn and roared, "Hoh, hoh! So now you have met the young ladies, my boy! Hah! Put the coffee on, Mama, and we'll all have a bite to eat. Hoh, hoh!"

While Mrs. L. prepared the coffee, Joe told us in rapid, run-together sentences, all about his trip from the prairie in his small roadster. Auntie listened breathlessly from the kitchen, and uncle smoked and laughed and prodded Joe for more details of the great journey. The account went on all through coffee and, by the time we were ready to leave, we knew to the minute just when Joe had arrived at, and de-

57

parted from, every point along the way, and what he had eaten at every stop. But he gallantly offered to drive us home, so we all piled into the little car, took off with a colossal lurch, and sizzled up the road at a speed that is sheer suicide on those twists and turns and kinks and holes.

So — this is Joe! Well, of course, he could be handsomer of face and of physique, and more interesting of speech — *but* — he has a *car*. And it's a long trek from Brilliant, so . . .

THURSDAY, NOVEMBER 14

I have seen an apparition! And I have talked with it! After school, I opened the door in answer to a knock. I beheld a female (I think — yes, I'm sure!) spectre — a scrawny, grubby one, so emaciated that she looked as though she had been through the ravages of all the horrors in the old red medical book, but from whose presence now even the littlest germ would run screaming. With a horrid grin that revealed her jagged, green teeth, she announced that her name was Olga Popoff. She was very noticeably pregnant, and shivered pitifully in a most inadequate coat. Against my better judgment, I had to ask, "Would you like to come in and get warm, Mrs. Popoff?"

"Shure; me vyery holodnoi — cold, cold," she croaked. "But me no meesus. Me jos' Olga. No meesus, me."

"Oh!" I replied, somewhat abashed, and feeling that I should add, "pardon *me!*"

She ambled in, gaping with unfeigned admiration at what must have appeared to her my very elegant rooms, and proceeded to remove her dirty plutok, coat, and muddy shoes, while I wondered wildly whether she had decided to stay permanently. Her hair was a disorderly mat of greasy black strings, apparently uncombed and unwashed for months. Her brown eyes darted and skimmed like swallows, and she grimaced continually. The cotton dress she wore was ragged and filthy, and black-rimmed toe nails protruded from the holes in her bunchy pink stockings. She stretched her feet towards the stove and grinned ecstatically as she mumbled, "Ni-ice! Ni-ice house," and rubbed first one foot, and then the other.

"Where do you live, Olga?" I asked, to make conversation and also because, not having seen her before, I was curious as to which village she lived in.

"Up far. Far up," she jerked out. "T'ree mile far."

"Did you walk down, or have you a horse and wagon?"

"Shure. Me walk. Me want see scholnitsa."

"Oh. Did you want to see me about something special?" I asked, hoping not, and wondering what on earth it could be.

"Shure!" she squeaked. "And you weell buy for me sawmeteeng Nyelson?"

"Well," I hedged, "I don't have a great deal of room in my suitcase, you know." I had visions of her making a request for me to try to obtain the wherewithall for an abortion! However, I needn't have worried on that score.

She grinned, and rasped, "And dis I need ees not for your suitcase hyeavy. So you weell breeng for me?"

"Well, I'll tell you after I know what it is," I countered.

A cunning look came into her wild eyes as she leaned forward and whispered hoarsely, "Powder! Powder me need! Pyink powder. And rooge! and lypistyick! And perfoom — roses perfoom!"

Poor shivering thing. Not a decent article of clothing on her — broken shoes, no rubbers, no gloves on her coarse red hands — and she yearned for cosmetics! I longed to suggest soap and water instead.

"And you weell gyet for me Nyelson?" she pleaded.

"Yes, I suppose so," I answered, though not too willingly, for I wondered where the money would come from for these ridiculous purchases.

"Good, good!" she grated. "Dyen me vyery preetty!"

I felt mean and uncharitable when I asked, "Did you bring me money for these things, Olga?"

"Oh, byad me!" and she clicked her tongue, and shook her head in self-recrimination. "Me forgyet mawney. Oh, byad me! And me breeng mawney Mawnday, okay?"

"Alright. I'll get them for you. Are you going back home now?" I asked, by way of suggestion.

To my immense relief, she fell in with my proposal, answering, "Shure. Me go home now. Fawder-my wait home."

"Oh, your father lives with you, does he?" I asked.

"And no. I lyive wit' fawder-my. Fawder-my, and brawder, too."

"I've never seen you before, Olga. I guess if you live a long way off, you don't come down here often."

"No. Styay home now lawtsa," she said, as she winked evilly and patted her swollen body. "Me gonna myarried soon," she confided. "And dot's good, huh?"

"Yes," I agreed, "that's very good. Well, good-bye Olga," I hurried to say before she went into any sordid details on the subject of her pregnancy.

MONDAY, NOVEMBER 18

Olga arrived at three o'clock sharp to collect her treasures, as cold and grubby and cheerful as before. She grinned more broadly than ever when I gave her the package, and she bobbed up and down in her excitement. As she prepared to leave, I reminded her, "Your powder and things were eighty-five cents, Olga." Needless to say, I had shopped at the dime store and bought the smallest sizes in all items.

"Oh, shure," she said, as she began fumbling in the front of her dress. She produced an untidy wad of stuff which she handed to me, saying "Me myake for you rawg."

It was a lumpy, lop-sided mat about a foot in diameter, made from dirty rags braided and sewn haphazardly into this semblance of the rugs that most women make. However, this one was unique in that the edges curled sharply upwards until it looked more like a shallow bag.

"Vyery nice rawg, huh?" Olga babbled.

"Yes, thank you very much," I said, with what I hoped sounded like pleasure in spite of the fact that I knew, now, that I'd been took!

Olga had known it right from the beginning, the scheming wretch! She looked victorious as she said, "Me myake for you. Dou'hobor lyadies myake like dot rawgs for eighty-five cyents. Myake house vyery preetty. Good-bye."

And she was gone with the speed of an antelope, leaving me literally holding the bag. Oh well, I thought, what's the difference? She's more happy than she's ever been before in her whole life, I'm sure, and there's no denying that wits like hers deserve *some* reward. And, fearing bugs and larvae and germs and bacteria and viruses and bacilluses, I dropped the Thing into the fire, and made a beeline for the disinfectant.

TUESDAY, NOVEMBER 19

Peg has been teaching "All Through the Night" to her class. At noon she heard one of her beginners singing haltingly to himself as he colored a picture, "Shleep, my chyile, an' peess all t'rough da night."

First snow today and it's the wet, sloppy kind that makes one wish that it were April. All the gloomy villages, with their clutters of sheds and barns, look more desolate than ever.

We have all been busy preparing for our Christmas concerts. In this part of the country, a concert means much more than just training the pupils. There are all the costumes to make, and that is the lot of the teacher, not, as in other communities, of doting mothers. In the first place, these women have not the slightest idea of what is required; secondly, they haven't the materials with which to make them; and thirdly, they have no time for such frivolities. Therefore, it is up to the teachers to not only contrive the costumes, but also to provide the necessary materials.

It is difficult to find parts for all the youngsters — and naturally they all wish to take part, since this is the biggest event in their dreary lives — for marches, drills, and dances are forbidden, the first two being military training, and the last an unpardonable sin. I have partially solved the problem by choosing a simplified version of Dickens' "A Christmas Carol" since so many can take part in that flexible play. The others will do songs — unaccompanied, of course, since music is the work of the devil — recitations, and acrostics.

WEDNESDAY, NOVEMBER 20

Decided to make our Castlegar trip right after school today. Luck was with us for as we passed Lipinski's, Joe came hurtling out and yelled, "Hey, where-ya-going?" We told him, and that beautiful, handsome male shouted in his rapid-fire way, "Well-for-goodness'-sakes-wait-a-minute-till-I-get-my-coat-and-I'll-drive-you-over," and before we knew it, we were on our way.

When we entered the store, we found Mr. Duchak making up books and Elsa behind the counter gazing out at Joe, who had remained in the car. Mr. Duchak came forward at once and welcomed us with, "Well, young ladies, it's nice to see you. I guessed I missed you last week. Elsa, do make some tea; these young ladies must be cold."

We thanked him, but said that we couldn't stay this time. Elsa, too entranced to look relieved at our refusal, asked with a great deal of interest, especially for Elsa, "Who is that man who brought you over?"

For Elsa to speak to us voluntarily, and civilly, is quite an innovation. But there's a man (of sorts) involved now, and we suspect that a little interest in, and by! genus homo is just what Elsa needs to perk her up. We told her about Joe, and she replied, "Oh, I know the Lipinskis a little. I must go over and see them some time soon."

Hah! Witness the Awakening of Elsa!

Upon our return to the car, Joe hailed us as though we'd been gone for at least a month and suggested that since, on the way over, Peg had sat in the middle and I on Gertie's knee, we should now change around. So going back, Gertie sat next to Joe and Peg on my lap.

As we approached Lipinski's, Mrs. L. came to the door waving a dishtowel at us and called, "Come on in, my loves, all of you. The supper is ready almost and you girls must stay. You simply must!" (just as though we had argued!)

We trooped into the kitchen which smelled like a dream and set us all a-drool with expectation. The table was laid with a red-and-white checked cloth, Mrs. L's best china, and

a bouquet of paper flowers. Joe bounced around us helping
us with our coats, nudging and poking us all in succession,
and with each jab he issued a loud p-s-s-st! the first of
which startled us almost beyond recovery. He whooped, and
auntie giggled, and said, "Oh you Joe, such a boy for fun!"
We had to giggle too, out of politeness, so then Joe p-s-s-st-ed
again and auntie giggled again and we giggled again, and
soon we were all a tittering, p-s-s-st-ing, wheeling, jumping
knot of morons. Mrs. L. wiped her streaming eyes on her
apron and gasped, "Oh my, my! Such fun since Joe comes
to us! Now, you all go in the front room and have more
fun till Papa comes in."

She wouldn't let us help her in the kitchen, so there was
nothing for it but to trail the cavorting Joe into the living
room. We would all have preferred to help Papa scoop
manure out of the barn but we had no say in the matter.
Joe started the gramophone and proceeded to thump his
feet, snap his fingers, and click his tongue in time, more
or less, to the music. We smiled appreciatively, examined
our fingernails, and brushed non-existent lint off our slacks.
When the record was finished, Joe blared, "Aw-that's-too-
tame-for-me-how-about-this-one," slapped another record on,
and yanked the unsuspecting Peg to her feet with sufficient
force to dislocate her spine. He whirled her around and
around the small floor space, missing the rubber plant by
inches, and scattering the hooked rugs to the four winds.
Gertie and I laughed and sang feverishly, and tapped our
feet, and clapped our hands, and the vases clattered, and
the whole house trembled. Such FUN! Auntie looked in
from the kitchen, waggled her head, and chuckled at the
sight of Young Things having a Good Time. When the music
stopped and Peg had reeled to a chair, Mrs. L. said in loving
tones, "Joe, you go now out and see if Papa is finished.
Tell him to hurry or the supper will be spoiled."

Away he went with a wink for Peg, a companionable
pat on the shoulder for Gertie, a friendly nudge in the ribs
for me, and a co-operative p-s-s-st to be shared by all three
of us. (Whatever else gives with Joe, he *is* fair). His aunt
said, "Ah, that Joe! Such a lively boy, and such a good
boy. Always making fun. Such a happy boy!"

Before we could reply, Joe bounded in with his uncle in tow and said cleverly, "See-I-always-get-my-man-just-like-the-Mounties-I-always-get-my-man." Everyone howled with appreciation and Mr. Lipinski boomed, "Joe, Joe, such a one you are! Hoh, hoh hoh!"

Supper proceeded then, after Joe had playfully flicked the hand towel at all of us in turn. He kept up a steady patter all through the delicious meal, and when it was over we forcibly pushed Mrs. L. into the living room and we four started the dishes. Peg washed, Gertie and I dried, and Joe put them away; never for a moment did he forget his role as star performer of the Lipinski Supper Club. He juggled dishes, he warbled and whistled, he twittered and hummed, he stamped and whirled — and he p-s-s-st-ed. I have never been so perilously close to a nervous breakdown. But he drove us home, which was most fortunate for us since we wouldn't have had the strength to walk. I sat next to Joe, and Gertie sat on Peg's lap.

We all slept here and, while preparing for bed, we compared the number of black-and-blue marks on our rib-sections. We each have nine.

SUNDAY, NOVEMBER 24

Have been recuperating from Wednesday's orgy and too weak to write anything. Had John and Mike and several others come calling on Thursday night.

When we passed Lipinski's this afternoon on our way up, a curtain was drawn back and *Elsa* waved at us! And Joe, the stinker, didn't come out and offer us a ride.

But at least our having to walk postponed the unpleasant discovery we made upon arrival here. When I went to get out the coffee tin, I noticed that several things had disappeared from my cupboard — a jar of walnuts, a package of dates, a can of pineapple, a tin of peanut butter, and several other items. Someone has been in during the week-end — but how? My windows are all locked, my door lock is a Yale, the door between the schoolroom and my quarters is bolted from this side, and I always lock the schoolroom windows and door at night, and when I leave. There is no outside entry-way into the cellar, so *how* did the thief get in?

It remains a mystery and a most disquieting one. It gives me an attack of the jitters every time I think of someone having been in, and I can't help wondering whether the sneak may some night think I am over at Ootischenia and come in by mistake while I'm asleep — if I ever sleep again, that is!

And besides the fact that I am once more petrified with fear, it makes me plain mad to haul provisions all this way only to have them stolen.

WEDNESDAY, NOVEMBER 27

Had supper with Peg and Gertie last night. They have fitted their coal-oil lamp with one of the new unbreakable chimneys, which has practically reduced poor Mrs. Makaoff to a state of prostration. She came in with a bowl of apples last evening and Peg, who was polishing the glass, called, "Here, catch," at the same time tossing the chimney at her and deliberately mis-aiming. Mrs. Makaoff saw that she couldn't possibly catch it and, with stark horror on her face, observed it on its way to the floor. She covered her eyes with her hands and let out a piercing shriek. It was so funny to watch her peer out between her fingers at what she thought would be wreckage, and to see her expression change from fear to consternation, to wonder, to disbelief, to joy — all in the space of seconds.

To these people a broken lamp is a matter of no small concern since a new one costs all of fifteen or twenty cents. But Mrs. Makaoff has now seen the most revolutionary discovery of the age and she expressed her awe and wonder in an oft-repeated, "Eh-h-h, good, good! Eh-h-h!"

6.30 — We're off to Castlegar and Lipinski's. I suggested that we don barrel staves under our sweaters in order to have some measure of protection against another possible onslaught by Joe, but Gertie thought we'd look misshapen. I can't see that it's better to be a pulpy black-and-blue has-been, but we don't know where there are any barrels anyway.

THURSDAY, NOVEMBER 28

Elsa was much more pleasant last night and we see faint traces of the glow of love (we think) upon her. She had two new dips in her hair and asked, "How are *all* the Lipinski's?" As though she didn't know, the hussy.

When we arrived at Brilliant, it was Joe himself who whipped the door open, made a deep bow to the floor with one hand on his round stomach and the other on his round posterior, then spun like a whirling dervish and p-s-s-st-ed with a poke, a jab, and a dig, and howled, "Hi-ya-hi-ya-where-ya-been-long-time-no-see-p-s-s-st!"

We didn't stay long because Mrs. Lipinski seemed a bit cool-ish (and made no move to put the coffee on) but while she wrapped our eggs and butter, Joe supplied his usual brand of entertainment. When we couldn't hang around any longer waiting for the snack invitation which was obviously not forthcoming, Joe bellowed, "Wait-a-minute-till-I-get-my-coat-and-I'll-drive-you-up."

After we were packed in the car he said sorrow- f u l l y, "I-sure-woulda-drove-you-up-on-Sunday-but-Auntie-had-company-and-I-couldn't-leave."

Ah-hah! 'Twas Auntie who had the company then, and not Joe. Auntie has told us more than once what a fine husband Joe would make, but now she probably feels that Elsa would be a much better choice than one (or all!) of us. And she's so right. Maybe that's why the withdrawn attitude tonight — and the empty coffee pot. Could it be, we wonder, that Auntie is now setting bait for Elsa and wishes to discourage prolonged visits by us? Joe didn't seem very happy at being kept in on Elsa's account, but we shall see, we shall see . . .

FRIDAY, NOVEMBER 29

Yesterday after school Gertie came in on her way to the bus. She had received a message at noon, by tele-phone, relayed to her by one of the boys who had been down to Brilliant, that she was needed at home. So I went over to Ootischenia to keep Peg company. Gertie arrived back at a little after midnight, having driven out in a borrowed car which she parked right at the door.

This morning at 6:30, when only Gertie was up (her turn to get breakfast), she heard a rap at the door, and there was Old Mike with an assortment of vegetables. Having spotted the car outside, he was most curious — and most suspicious, it developed. When he peered over Gertie's shoulder into the room and saw *two* humps in Peg's bed, where only *one* belonged, his eyes gleamed, Gertie said later, and he licked his chops with relish at his discovery of this disgraceful setup. Still gaping wide-eyed at the bed, where Peg and I slept on in delicious oblivion, Mike leered, "Ah-hah! Car-a outside! Hm-m! Ah-hah! Hm-m. Barclitch gottit *myan* shleeping! Eh-h-h, no good, no good, sawme kinda byad! Eh-h-h, vyery byad!"

It was at this point that Peg and I received our rude awakening. Gertie lunged over to the bed, shook us cruelly, and screeched, "Sit up! Sit up, you two! For heaven's sake, SIT UP!"

The sight of our two tousled heads dispelled Mike's relish and ruined his day, I am sure, but he gallantly rumbled, "Oh-h-h — just scholnitsa! Oh-h-h! Dot's awright, dot's awright, you shleep."

But how could anyone ever sleep again after one look at Mike! He is a grizzly, grimy old relic exuding a blended aroma of garlic, sweat, and urine. Grey straggly hair crowns his long horse-face, which has more dirt-encrusted grooves than a boy's hands in marble-playing season. A wispy moustache, streaked grey and yellow, hangs dejectedly over his mouth like a tattered curtain. His trousers, the like of which I have never seen before, are shiny with a slick coating of greasy streaks and spots from every meal he has eaten since his birth, and are so rigid that they would stand at attention even if he were not occupying them. As a final flourish, the fly is minus all but two or three buttons, and I was alternately fascinated and repulsed, wondering just how much longer it will be before these remaining vestiges of decency give up the struggle in disgust and decamp from their unlovely location. And what then, oh horrible thought?

He gasps and wheezes as though each breath were his last, and between the wheezes interpolates fervent prayers thus: "Oh-h-h, ah-h-h! Oh-h hospidi, hospidi! Oh-h-h shyit! Ah-h-h, whee-e-e-e, oh-h-h, hospidi! Ah-h-h, sh-sh-IT!"

The girls tell me that he suffers from some respiratory ailment and pays them with vegetables for the medicine they buy for him in town. Apparently they are not worried that he will expire on their doorstep for they didn't shoo him off, but I'm glad he isn't in *my* precinct.

After Mike had left, I had Gertie and Peg convulsed with laughter at the account of the Ostrakoff grandmother, who also has an ailment. Apparently she has been feeling miserable for some time, so last week her son took her to town to see a doctor. The other day he passed Pleasant and I asked him how his mother was. He scratched his head and answered, "Wyell, I dunno yet for shure. You see, she got sawme kinda trouble — she didn't shyits enawgh. So I'm tyelling da doctor, and he say she should tyake sawme kinda cyastor oil. So now she's gonna tyake like dot, and we'll see wot she's gonna gyet."

I'm not sure, but I *think* I replied, "Oh, that'll be lovely. I hope she gets la-a-wtsa!"

DECEMBER

SUNDAY, DECEMBER 1

CAME out from town to-night through six inches of fresh snow to find that literally every edible morsel, canned and otherwise, has disappeared from my cupboard. If there is any comfort or satisfaction in the discovery, we do know now how the thief gets in. He removes the Yale lock completely! We found traces of shavings and sawdust on the floor and a little split in the casing near the lock. So I guess I might just as well leave the door wide open from now on, and all my groceries in a basket on the table for easier removal. We have not the slightest idea as to who the culprit could be — and short of staying here in the dark for an entire weekend, can think of no way to find out.

For some time now I have been making a purchase for various of the women at a Nelson drug store. Each one hands me a slip of paper with the one word, "Rustwa" written upon it, and her interpreter instructs me to "buy dis in drog store Nyelson." Which I have done quite cheerfully although the clerk, whom I know by sight only, has, I must admit, looked at me a bit curiously. Last Saturday I shopped for this item again and while I waited for him to wrap it, I asked, "Just what is this 'rustwa'?"

He glanced up sharply, blushed and coughed and cleared his throat, and finally replied, "Why, it's - er - ah - well, it's a solutionforthepurposeofcontra . . ."

Before he could finish, the light dawned—"It's—OH! Oh my! Oh dear me! You don't say! Er—oh! Isn't this a lovely day? I mean, what a blizzard we're having, didn't you? Er . . ."

His look said, much more loudly than words, "TRAMP!"

He was completely disgusted with me, *Miss* Hulls, strolling in there every second or third weekend and brazenly buying rustwa; and now, to cover up my sinful life, I put on an act by simpering, "What is this 'rustwa'?"

As I hastily scooped up the infernal package and slithered out with seven shades of magenta crawling over my face, I just knew that he snorted to himself, "Who's she think she's kidding?"

If he ever chats with the clerk at the Court House, she'll likely tell him that I didn't get away with it, and he'll add that I had it coming. *Such situations!*

Mike called after the girls had left, and told me more about his intentions to leave the community and live his own life. But I wasn't prepared when he said, "And I think you and I could do pretty good together, Miss Hulls."

I'm not quite sure now just how I got out of that one, but in the light of what people are probably saying about me in Nelson right now — that is, those who know the gal at the Court House and the guy at the drug store — it is just possible that I would be wise to accept Mike and clothe myself in the robe of respectable marriage.

WEDNESDAY, DECEMBER 4

When we went to Duchak's last night there was no Elsa to be seen, but when we reached Lipinski's we found out why. Elsa was there, of course. She and Joe sat on the slippery sofa looking at snapshots and Joe didn't p-s-s-st once, although he looked as though he'd burst if he couldn't let go soon. Elsa had the cat-that-swallowed-the-canary mien, and Auntie hovered over them, and beamed, and didn't say anything about coffee. So, hungry and thirsty and cold, we trudged up the snowy road and called Joe names for not having fortitude enough to up and give us a ride home. He was not enjoying himself one whit with Elsa, and we know that he'd much have preferred to jump up and yell, "Wait-a-minute-till-I-get-the-car-out-and-I'll-drive-ya-home."

And we aren't conceited either. It bodes no good, we fear, for Joe.

71

THURSDAY, DECEMBER 5

It poured buckets all day to-day. Sloshed over to Ootischenia after school and found Gertie and Peg both marking
books in Gertie's classroom. Since they had only a few left
to do, I glanced through a magazine while waiting for them.
There was no sound except that of a page turning occasionally, the hiss of the lamp, and the rain on the roof. But
simultaneously we all suddenly became aware of a monoto-
nous tick-tick-tick somewhere in the room. We listened, and
it went on as regularly as a clock. Gertie said, "It sounds
like a clock, but I have no clock in here," whereupon Peg
leaped up, shrieking, "A clock! My gosh! That's just what
it is! Come on, let's get out! Hurry!"

"But why?" I asked mystified that she should be so upset
at the mention of something as harmless as a clock.

"Come on, stupid," she said shakily. "Don't you know
that those devils set off bombs with a clock? Hurry up before
it goes off!"

Gertie picked up the lamp and we started for the door.
The tick-tick-tick grew louder, so we knew that we were
getting closer to the bomb. It was near the door, then — but-
but-but that door was our only exit. We held our breaths and
prayed that we might get out before the barn came crashing
down around our ears. I was wishing I'd stayed at Pleasant
and married Mike, when Gertie began guffawing. I thought
she had become the victim of hysterics and would have
slapped her face, like they do in the movies, but I was afraid
she would drop the lamp and set fire to the place even before
the bomb exploded. Then Peg and I saw her pointing at a
puddle near the door. From a hole in the roof came a steady
tick-tick-tick, only now it sounded more like drip-drip-drip.

Which proves that not only does the quickness of the
hand deceive the eye, but so also does the regularity of the
drip confuse the ear and distort what is left of the mind.

We had just reached the house when one of Gertie's
pupils, Nellie Evdokimoff, came screaming through the rain,
"Meess Meelne, Meess Meelne, and you mawst cawme queeck
to our plyace. And Syam was myad at Weellie and Weellie
was byending over and Syam was t'rowing a knife at Weellie

and now Weellie hyave da knife een hees ass and you mawst cawme, mawder say, and pooll out da knife. Queeck, Meess Meelne! And mawder say you mawst hurry op!"

"Teaching is such a dignified profession," THEY said at Normal. Let's see THEM pull a knife out of Willie's — dignified! Hmph!

FRIDAY, DECEMBER 6

Heard the most blood-curdling noises over at Ootischenia last night. They came from some distance away and the girls said it was John Argotoff, a poor wretched, imbecilic youth who, the children say, is kept penned in an enclosure by day, and chained at night. We *hope* that this is a true fact, for if his appearance and mentality are in keeping with his dreadful howls, one sight of him would send us running for Nelson.

SUNDAY, DECEMBER 8

Peg and Gertie didn't come home this weekend. I was on my way out to the road on Friday evening, and not relishing the thought of that three-mile walk alone in the absolute darkness, when John (Markin, *not* Argotoff) loomed out of the night and offered to carry my bag down for me. I felt most grateful to him for his kindness and said so. He apparently seized the moment for what it was worth because suddenly I realized that he had said, "And I sure like to help you, Miss Hulls. I wouldn't mind to help you all my life, if you would let me."

Two proposals — for that's what they are — in one week are almost more than I can bear. I wonder if John and Mike have a bet on? Or whether they are both light-headed at the intoxicating dream of what wonders could be accomplished with my salary? After all, thirty — maybe even *forty* — dollars every month . . .

TUESDAY, DECEMBER 10

Peg and Gertie came over for supper, and then we went on our weekly shopping expedition on Tuesday, instead of Wednesday — with a purpose.

73

On the way down, Peg told us her latest story. She had caught Johnny Pookachoff doing what he had to do against the school wall instead of in the proper place. True, that's about all the walls of the barn are good for, but still . . . As punishment, she had ordered him to make fifty round trips after school between school and the privy, and she sat at her desk marking 1 - 2 - 3 as Johnny made each complete circuit. He had reached the neighborhood of 30 when his grandmother arrived in a terrible fury, waving her arms and shouting angrily. On his next trip around, Johnny explained tearfully that his grandmother wanted him home at once to feed the cow and get his wood in. Peg instructed him to tell the old lady why he was being detained. This he did, in Russian, whereupon grandmother removed her shawl and flapped it at Johnny, yelling, "Byad, byad!" The culprit resumed his travels, but now he had an added insult to bear, for each time he came through the room, the old grandmother swatted at him with the shawl and screeched at him in Russian.

Elsa was on hand in the store and asked anxiously whether we had walked or ridden over from Brilliant. We put her mind at rest by saying we'd walked, and she was so relieved that when Mr. Duchak suggested tea just then, she frowned only slightly. But she put the kettle on — which was the main thing. Peg asked her how she was feeling and she replied, "Oh, I'm not too bad *now*," and she was almost civil to us for the half hour we were there.

We had a feeling that Elsa would rather we'd stick to our usual Wednesday night for calling at Lipinski's, instead of altering our schedule as we had. But this was our purpose: we wanted to see whether Joe would perform in his old rambunctious style when Elsa was not around. And had we gone on Wednesday, as usual, and as expected, we're quite sure that Elsa would have "happened" to be there. (Hah, me proud beauty, now we shall see).

We saw. And we had guessed correctly. Joe danced and jiggled and cheeped and poked and p-s-s-st-ed and nudged and patted. Auntie looked very disapproving (and didn't offer to make coffee), but Joe whooped, "Wait-a-minute-till-I-put-water-in-the-car-and-I'll-drive-ya-home." Auntie scowled and said that the road was pretty slippery. (You too, Auntie).

So now we know. Mrs. L. is set on a match between Joe and Elsa, and she just doesn't want us around to mess things up. Poor Joe, to be saddled with Elsa! Poor US! . . . We have seen the handwriting on the wall and the beginning of the end of these life-saving rides. Ho hum.

FRIDAY, DECEMBER 13

Had John and his guitar on Wednesday night, and Mike and his mandolin last night. By keeping each plunking steadily at his instrument, and begging for more every time the "music" stopped, I forestalled any further comments —if there were any more in cold storage — on the subject of marriage.

MONDAY, DECEMBER 16

Gertie and Peg over for supper. At noon Peg was strolling towards the who's-it and being kept at close range by several of her little girls — which is always the case when any of us venture outside. When she entered her place of destination, they stopped a short distance off to await her reappearance. After a moment or two she heard all conversation cease as one of them said, in a loud whisper, "Sh-h, and teacher ees peessing!"

Even our humblest acts are regarded with reverence and awe by our adoring pupils!

WEDNESDAY, DECEMBER 18

We are skipping the Castlegar-Brilliant trip this week since school will be out on Friday for the Christmas vacation.

Excitement has been increasing by leaps and bounds as concert time draws near, until I fear that something (probably me) will explode before to-morrow night, the date for the momentous occasion.

It is now 2:30 a.m. and I think I can go to bed at last. The costumes are all ready, including the one for Paul Ozeroff who will play the role of that beloved Saint Nicholas. Apparently the children have not had a Santa Claus for years, and they were wild with delight when I announced that he would likely call to-morrow evening. I suspect that some, if not all of them, know who it is going to be, but they are enjoying the delightful suspense to the utmost by pretending that they do not know it will be anyone but Saint Nick in the flesh. I would have asked either John or Mike to do the honors, but couldn't ask the one without offending the other, so decided this would be the best way out.

There is a small gift from me to each pupil, and a bag of candies and nuts for each. These arrived in bulk a few days ago and I had a confusing and sticky two hours arranging them in the bags. Each one must contain the same number, kind, and color of candies; I learned this at Hallowe'en when I saw the children comparing the contents of their bags and heard such comments as, "Eh-h-h, and you got t'ree blyack ones and here's only two in my byag!" and "Lookit! John got seven yellow cyandies and Myary hyave nine."

The Christmas tree stands grand and imposing in a corner of the schoolroom, and is the object of day-long awe and admiration. When I asked my pupils a week ago to bring decorations for the tree, they all said that they had none, since Christmas trees are not a tradition in their homes as they are in ours. So I brought yards of glittering tinsel, and boxes of glass ornaments and icicles from home. When I brought them into the room, the youngsters caught their breaths at such splendor, and burst into a chorus of ah's and oh's and e-h-h-'s. For the past few days I have watched them stand before the tree and reverently touch a shining ball or finger a tinsel garland. Children before a Christmas tree are always a joy to watch, but these beauty-starved waifs are enthralled beyond all reason, and the look in their eyes as they worship this tree makes me all lump-in-the-throatish. So that they might have a part in the decorations, I gave them colored paper and they made yards of chains, and dozens of cutout figures, and hung them so thickly on the tree that there are scarcely any branches visible.

So now all is ready for this breathtaking event. Whether anyone will remember any of his lines remains to be seen,

but even if no one says a word from the stage, I don't think it will matter; there will still be the tree to exclaim over.

FRIDAY, DECEMBER 20—2 a.m.

Never again! I am positively haggard. I am reduced to an inanimate rag, bone, and hank of hair. I am a dragged-out lump, and there is simply nothing else in the world but my tiredness.

It started at exactly 5:25 yesterday afternoon when I heard a commotion outside, followed by an insistent knocking at my door. There stood fifteen or twenty of my excited pupils wanting to know whether "eet ees time yet."

"No," I said coldly, "it is *not* time yet. It isn't even half past five and I told you all not to come before seven o'clock."

"But you know, Meess Hulls, and we weell cawme in da school and hyelp you," said the spokesman.

"No, Mike," I replied, seeing the uncontrollable excitement in them. "Thank you just the same, but none of you would be of any help just now, because the things left to be done can be done only by myself."

"And we could just be in da school and wyait," he persisted, and a volley of shouts encored this wonderful suggestion:

"Shure, Meess Hulls!"

"Any you weell lyet?"

"And we would just syit in da school."

I knew that they were in no state of mind to just sit *anywhere*, least of all in the schoolroom, and I felt heartless as I refused, but I simply had to have at least another hour to work uninterrupted. I closed the door and started in a frenzy to do the dozen little jobs still not completed. The racket outside was deafening as they pushed and scuffled and shouted in their need to let off steam; and if I'd had a supply of chloroform on hand, I would most certainly have tossed a couple of pints over them.

It was not later than six o'clock when I was again summoned to the door, this time by Nicky Stoochnoff with a sad lament. "And Meess Hulls, granmawder-my hyave her feet cold, and she want to go een da school."

"Well, Nicky," I said, with not the slightest sympathy, "your grandmother should not have come so early. All of you know that the concert isn't till half-past seven," and once more closed the door.

Ten minutes later he was back. "And Meess Hulls, granmawder-my hyave her feet *vyery* cold now and she want to go een da school."

My patience was wearing very thin by this time, and my temper was straining at its leash; I had had nothing to eat yet; and I had told the children a dozen times not to come before seven o'clock. Blast it, I hoped they'd all freeze to death out there, every last grandmother and father and uncle of them! Couldn't they understand that I just could not have them all in the schoolroom charging around for a full hour before the programme? Hadn't the parents and grandparents any sense at all? If it were one grandmother and one or two youngsters, I could allow them in, but I peeked out and saw what looked like hundreds of men, women, and children. The adults shouted back and forth at one another, babies howled, and the school-age contingent chased one another furiously around the crowd, ducking in and out, and upsetting younger children.

At 6:25 Paul Ozeroff arrived to find out whether it was time to don the Santa Claus suit. As I restrained myself from hitting him with the poker, I reminded him that I'd said he needn't get ready until nine o'clock and he said, "I thought maybe I should get ready a little bit earlier, just to be sure."

At 6:30 Larien Zaitsoff came to announce, "And Meess Hulls, my leettle syister she is crying and it is start to snow and da people askit you weell lyet to go in da school?"

I gave up. I couldn't get anything done anyway with these ten-minute interruptions, and if they tore the place down it no longer mattered. In they trooped, scores and scores of them. There couldn't have been a living soul left at home, for the crowd included the tiniest babies and the oldest, frailest grandparents. The parents and old people were as excited as the children, and violent pandemonium broke out as they all shouted, and pushed, and buffeted one another in their eagerness to get in. I had had visions of being the gracious teacher extending a welcoming hand to each as they entered, but I found myself instead cowering in a corner to avoid being trampled to death. The school children hollered and pointed out the decorations and the tree; parents unbundled their writhing, squawking babies; grandparents jabbered at each other in loud tones of wonder, and the noise, swelled to a mighty crescendo. I ducked into my kitchen and bolted a sandwich, and wished that I'd failed at Normal School.

At last it was 7:30 and, doubting whether I could stay sane for another two hours, I made a little speech of welcome to which nobody listened. Even when the programme started, the din continued — though with slightly less volume. While children performed, their baby sisters and brothers trailed around after them and howled and gurgled intermittently. There was old Marley's ghost, with a bawling two-year-old sister hanging onto his coattails; and there a snowbird, with a creeping baby wailing up into her face; and there a Christmas fairy having her tinsel wings yanked askew by her beaming little cousin of three.

I dashed back and forth between the schoolroom and my kitchen and bedroom, which had become dressing-rooms. No one could find anything, and all had forgotten their lines and asked in frenzied choruses, "And Meess Hulls, I don't remyember what to say after . . ." and "I scyared to seeng," and "I poot my dryess here and now eet ees not here," and "Meess Hulls, I forgyet da syecond verse." I couldn't see that it mattered what they said onstage — or whether they said anything at all — because no one was listening anyway.

After an eternity, the programme was over and the stars of the evening began shouting about Santa Claus. I tore in to help Paul put the cushion in the right spot, and rushed back to be in the classroom when he should make his entrance from the outside. In he came with his pack, and he was magnificent. His was the one perfectly acted role of the entire evening, and his arrival caused the one silence of the entire proceedings. After the first surprise, the old people chortled and guffawed and poked one another; the children screeched with delight; the babies howled with fear. While Paul and I

distributed the gifts, boys and girls and toddlers milled about
like ants, and the tree swayed drunkenly on its base. When
the parcels had all been opened and e-h-h-ed over, everyone
began scrambling into coats and plutoks, and the noise was
louder than ever as children's fatigue was added to their
excitement.

At the door, those parents who can speak some English
repaid me for this nightmare when they beamed and said
"Vyery fine party!"

"Lawtsa good time. T'ank you very moch."

"Good, good. We cawme sawme more. You vyery good
teacher."

"Good-bye. Good-bye. Spusi hospidi."

"T'ank you, t'ank you. Spusi. Spusi hospidi. Vyery fine!"

I bolted the door and turned to view the battered corpse
which had once been my schoolroom. The desks were all
pushed this way and that; nut shells and orange peelings
were everywhere; the decorations hung in shreds on the
tree; parts of costumes lay anywhere and everywhere; and
over the entire floor was a thick carpet of sunflower-seed
husks.

The Doukhobors chew sunflower seeds constantly and it
used to fascinate me to watch their manipulation of these
tiny "nuts." They pop one into one side of the mouth, crack
goes the shell, out goes the husk from the other side of the
mouth, and at that exact moment another seed is popped in.
This crack-crunch-ptoo, crack-crunch-ptoo goes on and on
with the regularity and smooth motion of a pendulum, and
since all, young and old, chew them wherever they are, the
husks had to-night piled up to an amazing thickness.

I took one look at the shambles and decided that I just
couldn't start on the job of reconstruction to-night, so I went
into my kitchen and wilted onto the nearest chair. The chaos
in my rooms was almost as great, with costumes on chairs,
table, bed and floors, but the fire was on and I thought that
with my one remaining speck of life I could probably manage
to make a cup of coffee. Just then there was a rap at the
door and I almost broke into uncontrollable tears as I antici-
pated John or Mike. I opened the door, prepared to say that

I was too tired for any visitors, but instead of either of the boys I beheld two hollow-eyed, drooping wraiths — Peg and Gertie. They stumbled in, looked at me, and I at them, and without a word having been spoken, we all three burst into laughter. We laughed and laughed — and I am not sure that there weren't traces of hysteria in our howls. Over coffee and sandwiches we compared notes, and the bedlam had been as complete at Ootischenia as at Pleasant. We were all completely fagged but we felt just plain good, through and through, because everyone (except us) had had such a wonderful time.

I have an assortment of gifts from some of my pupils. These include three striped rectangular mats woven on hand looms; two oval braided mats; a very gaudy cushion; two embroidered dresser scarves; a wooden doorstop; eight crocheted doilies; a crocheted yoke of the sort that used to adorn what I believe were called "corset-covers" in the good old days; and two pairs of ankle socks, one pair in the usual Doukhobor blue, and the other white with pink and green stripes.

FRIDAY, DECEMBER 20

I doubt whether a mere two weeks' vacation will restore me to my former long-ago self, but here I go. I have removed my personal belongings to a nearby village as is the custom of teachers in Doukhobor schools during holidays, for one never knows what school will go up next, nor when. The litter has been cleared from the school room and it once more looks circumspect and decorous. The "take" of sunflower husks was seven large shovelsful!

MONDAY, DECEMBER 30—At Home

There were two items of considerable interest in this morning's paper. First, School Pleasant is no more! Late last night it was the target of a very thorough bombing and to-day lies in complete ruins. The inspector took me out to see it this afternoon, and if it were not for the sight of twisted desk frames, one would never guess what purpose the building had originally served. It is simply a jumbled pile of rubbish; the roof and walls lie in a million pieces on what is left of the floor, and splintered boards, shattered glass, and crumbled plaster cover the surrounding ground like confetti.

Apart from the inspector and myself, there was not another soul to be seen, and a peculiar hushed stillness pervaded the whole community. I don't know as yet where I'll be holding forth in the new term, but Peg and Gertie are in the same school-less state as I, the barn having been condemned by the Official Trustee for further use as a school.

The second item of note announced that Elsa, daughter of J. Duchak, had become the bride of Joseph, nephew of Mr. and Mrs. G. Lipinski! So between them, Auntie and Elsa have relegated the jubilant (heretofore) Joe to the safe status of blessed matrimony and nevermore, I betcha, will poor Joe dare to be his ebullient self. It's a downright shame. For us.

P-s-s-st, p-s-s-st, p-s-s-st . . . farewell!

JANUARY
OOTISCHENIA

SUNDAY, JANUARY 19

WE'RE back! And all three of us together! I love bombs
and I adore decrepit old barns, for now I need no longer
quiver and shake alone. Of course I shall probably have to
face up to a sharp deterioration in my hearing powers which,
over the past four months, have become extraordinary. I
have spent so many after-dark hours just listening . . . listening . . . that I can even hear a spider spinning his web — it
sounds like a freight train shunting; and I could, if it were
spring, hear a leaf popping out of its bud with a loud bang;
I know when a kitten, in a house a mile away, is stomping
about. This marvellous ability will no doubt now recede — but
— I shall be able to go to bed and *sleep*. I can scarcely wait.

In the past two weeks, workmen have been preparing
living quarters and schoolrooms for us, and now we are
ready to go again. We are ensconced on the top floor of the
Pictin house, where we have a large kitchen-living room
(contrived by the removal of the partition between two of
the "houses"), each a separate bedroom (Peg's complete
with cradle hook but no cradle), and an extra room for
storage. There is, of course, nothing as modern as plumbing
— we do not even have a water tap; we must haul water

84

from the kitchen downstairs. Then, after the water has been *used*, we must cart it down again for disposal. My schoolroom is in the big community kitchen, Gertie's in the front (wedding and funeral) room, and Peg's in the front room of the Faminoff house across the courtyard.

Our future safety has been guaranteed — or so the Trustee tells us. In the baseboard below each window in our "flat" has been installed a large iron ring with a stout rope attached to it. When we hear the first b'm of a bomb, or the initial crackle of a fire, we are to each clasp a rope in our hands, open the window, and shinny down to deliverance. This has all been very carefully and technically thought out and is a really peachy idea. We had practice to-night; that is, we practised holding the ropes and sitting on the window sills. That was as far as we could get. Instead of looking like Girls Escaping Death with daring and heroism, we merely resembled three monkeys perched on window ledges holding their tails in their hands and waiting for the organ grinder. So we threw the ropes out the windows and went downstairs to see whether we could get *up* by means of these lifelines. Had a little success, for we were each able to get about three feet off the ground. Of course, we realize that the ropes were not provided for the purpose of clambering *into* a bombed or burning house, but when we show our friends the snapshots taken of us three feet from the bottom, we hope they'll think we are on the way down and be properly awestruck at our dauntless courage.

On our way up to-night, we called in to wish happiness to Elsa and congratulations to Auntie. Oh, and to Joe. We can think of no reason why Joe should be congratulated, but it's etiquette and we seen our dooty and we done it, by cracky. Mrs. L. invited us in with traces of the friendliness she used to show us, and shouted for the bridal pair. They appeared, Elsa dragging the reluctant Joe by the hand. He looked as bewildered as a small boy awakened suddenly in the night. Passion Flower, tongue in cheek, looked pityingly down her long blue nose at us (poor virgin spinsters that we are) and masticated the canary which she is in the process of swallowing. Auntie should really be the bride in this setup;

85

she is the one who glows, sparkles, scintillates. She gave us all the details of the wedding — including the fact that Joe's new suit cost $48.95 — while Elsa looked coy and knowing, and Joe just plain miserable.

So that's that. Auntie doesn't seem to even notice that Joe is no longer "such a happy boy, always making fun." We don't expect to be going in often, for sure as guns Joe would sooner or later cut the traces, and all his pent-up jabs and pokes and nudges and p-s-s-sts would come tumbling out. Anyway, she'd never let him drive us home.

MONDAY, JANUARY 20

Classes were resumed to-day in our new schoolrooms. It's a much superior arrangement as far as grading is concerned, for now I have only grades four to eight, Gertie two and three, and Peg primary. This means a great deal less work for all of us, as well as more time for each teaching class.

While I taught this morning, Mrs. Pictin bumbled around at the back of the room making a great clatter with her bread-making procedure, and at the moment I said, "Now then, this is a copula verb," she thrust a great chunk of steaming bread into my hand. The grammar lesson was postponed until I had sampled the bread, smacked my lips, and rubbed my stomach appreciatively. One of the conditions under which the Pictins agreed to surrender their kitchen for a classroom was that they be allowed to use the oven. But this commotion will take place only about once a week, so I guess I can stand it.

We have worked out a system for cooking and dish-washing, by which each one of us will prepare one meal a day and she who cooks the meal does not do dishes. Methinks that I, at least, will add some weight for at Pleasant I had neither the time, nor the inclination, to cook proper meals.

We have also bestowed Russian names on one another since we now live in a village and are almost completely Doukhobor. Gertie is Hrunka (the closest we could come to

Gertrude), Peg is Marhutka (Margaret), and I am Hopka (Helen).

Another Safety Measure has been willed to us. Since the Poofing of Pleasant, we have been presented with a guard — a fat, dumpy old character who is almost entirely hidden beneath several layers of coats, sweaters, caps, and mufflers, and speaks nary a word, either English or Russian — at least to us. He has been provided with an ancient blunderbuss of doubtful-looking efficiency, and goes round and round the school all night long with his weapon slung over his shoulder on a strap.

WEDNESDAY, JANUARY 22

A veritable blizzard is under way and we had only a very few pupils to-day — those who live in this village and the one or two others nearest to the school. The classrooms were unbearably cold in spite of roaring fires, so we brought the youngsters upstairs and had games, stories, and riddles, and made candy. They were astounded when they tasted the finished product, and full of loud e-h-h's of admiration that we could accomplish such a wonderful feat as actually *making* candy! Several of the girls painstakingly, and in minute detail, wrote down the directions and announced that they were going to see "if mawder weell lyet to try at home."

Our poor old guard is on duty from dark until daylight and it is horribly cold out, so to-night we decided to call him in for a cup of tea and some hot biscuits, of which I had made a dozen or so. Peg leaned out of the window and called, "Hey! Come up and have some tea."

He stopped in his weary round, peered up through his layers of caps and mufflers, and grunted, "Huh?"

"Come on up here and get some tea."

"Huh?"

"We've made you some tea. Come up."

"Huh?"

"Come here. Up. Tea."

"Huh?"

"Tea! Hot tea!"

"Huh?"

"Chi!"

"O-o-h!"

And before she could get the window completely closed, he was up the stairs and sitting at the table. He neither looked at us nor spoke, but how he did slurp the scalding tea! And how he did swallow biscuits! He made the most fearful noises in the disposal of both, and left not a single biscuit. We had soda crackers with *our* tea after he had departed. I suppose his need was greater than ours, but must we always learn everything the hard way?

FRIDAY, JANUARY 24

The snow piled up in great drifts a mile high and the thermometer is a mile low, so we are not going home this weekend. We're going to eat, and sleep, and read, and knit, and write letters, and thoroughly enjoy ourselves. The prospect of a weekend at Pleasant, alone as I was, would have converted me into a hysterical hyena, but this one will be sheer pleasure.

Our "apartment" is not all that might be desired in the way of solid comfort, for the wind howls in around the windows, fluttering the curtains and blinds, and in the mornings we sweep snow off the inside ledges. However, by stoking furiously and arranging ourselves as close as possible to the stoves, we manage not too badly. We have the small heater from Peg's and Gertie's previous lodgings set up in hall, and it warms our bedrooms to some (small) extent. Mine was also salvaged, more or less battered, from the wreckage of Pleasant, and we have given it to Mr. Pictin to use in his cellar to protect the water pipes. We are now hauling our water up *two* flights of stairs from the cellar, since the ground floor pipes surrendered to the cold long ago.

The little heater saved our hides yesterday. Mr. Pictin demanded the right to store some things in one of the empty rooms up here, and to have a key to the outside door so that he could come in whenever he wished to go to the storeroom, whether we were here or not. Of course we refused. Our land-lord swelled up like a football, grew livid with rage, and roared, "And you lyet me to use dot room, I syay!"

"Sorry, Mr. Pictin, but we can't do that."

"I tyell you, you geeve me to use da room, you damn sawckers, or I gonna tyell gawverment!"

"No, you may not use the room. You knew when you rented these rooms that they were not for any use by you. Sorry, but it isn't possible."

"You geeve to use da room, I syay!" — this with some highly lurid, and unprintable, expletives.

"No. Sorry."

"Okay, I gonna show you! You don't lyet me to use da room, I don't lyet you to gyet water een my cellar. Now we're gonna see. Hah!"

"Okay, you don't let us get water from your cellar, we don't let you use our stove. Then your pipes will freeze. Mr. Pictin?"

So he keeps the stove and we get water. Hah!

MONDAY, JANUARY 27

A most restful weekend. We are reading "Gone With the Wind," taking turns at reading aloud and alternately hating, loving, and admiring Scarlett O'Hara. But Scarlett is no good for our housekeeping routine; we sit listening by the hour while the kettle boils dry, the dishes remain unwashed, the fires go out — and we suddenly realize that we are per-ishing in the cold.

Mike arrived this evening with bushels of mail, the first we have had since last Wednesday. This made him a hero and we repaid him with coffee and cake.

THURSDAY, JANUARY 30

We had Olga Popoff to see us today. She was well gar-nished with the powder, rouge, lyipstyick, and roses perfoom I had bought her, but otherwise unchanged — except for her pregnancy. She informed us that she had had her baby, a boy, but that she hadn't got married after all. Then she launched her next request: she wanted to borrow a suitcase and a coat from one of us — she didn't mind which. No favorites. Since none of us would ever again use anything Olga borrowed, and since we aren't affluent enough to make her an outright gift of either article, we had to refuse.

"But," I asked, "why do you need a coat and a suitcase, Olga? Are you moving away?"

She rolled her eyes, and giggled, and squirmed, as she replied, "Oh, me gonna gyet myarried now."

Peg said, "But I thought you and your man weren't getting married?"

She looked sly and cunning as she grinned and answered, "No, we don't gyet myarried. Not dot myan. Me got a new myan now."

We were amazed, wondering how a bad dream like Olga can go wandering around picking men off trees right and left. Gertie swallowed and asked, "Whom are you going to marry now, Olga?"

She scratched her head with one hand, and wiped her nose on the back of the other, and gurgled, "Me gonna myarry Beell."

"Bill?" queried Peg. "Bill who?"

This was very interesting, since we know a dozen Bills out here. But not Olga's Bill, I guess. Apparently she doesn't know him very well either. At any rate she answered, "Me dunno. But he's Beell sawme kinda." And she scratched again.

The plot thickens. I had another question: "Where did you meet Bill, Olga, and where does he live?"

Olga knew all the answers. "Me meet hyim lyast mawnt' on ryailway track," and she winked suggestively, "and he syay he lyive Shurragres. He syay he gonna myarry me."

Well, it looks as though Bill knew an easy mark when he saw one, but I'll wager that Olga won't be going to Shore-acres as *Mrs.* Bill. And furthermore, familiarity breeds contempt, they say — and also a lot of other things!

It was my turn to get supper to-night. Gertie has been agitating for apple pie, so I thought this would be a good time to make one. In order to get it into the oven as quickly as possible, I didn't waste time lighting the lamp, but went at the job instead in the late afternoon half light. The girls smacked their lips appreciatively when I produced my masterpiece at supper. But the lamp was lighted now, and when I cut the pie, we were all mystified to see it oozing a brilliant yellow juice. Fumbling away in the poor light, I had used curry instead of cinnamon. We had bread and jam for dessert.

FEBRUARY

MONDAY, FEBRUARY 3

MRS. Vereshagin has had Peg and Gertie breathing down a lawyer's neck since before Christmas. She is a widow with four children, and determined that she shall have the Widow's Pension, has been pestering the girls night and day to arrange this for her with the lawyer. This has been going on since before we moved over here, and they have been unable to make her understand that since she and her husband were married only by Doukhobor standards, and therefore not legally as far as law is concerned, she is not eligible for the pension. Goaded by constant pressure from Mrs. V., they said that they would try once more to get some kind of help for her. They saw the lawyer again on Saturday and naturally got the same reply as to the non-existence of a legal marriage, but he said that he would see what could be done about support for the children.

Last night, when we returned from town, she and her brood were here awaiting the latest report. It was a most tiresome session since, of course, Polly had to interpret everything that was said, and Peg told her at last in exasperation, "She might just as well forget about the widow's pension, Polly. Your mother did not have a legal marriage ceremony, and as far as law is concerned she was not married at all."

Polly repeated this ultimatum to her mother, whose eyes immediately blazed fire and whose tongue let loose such a screeching tirade that we feared she would burst on the spot. Polly reported that the import of the wordstorm had been, "And dot myan cryazy! Shure I myarried — lookit how moch keeds I got!"

A Doukhobor marriage is most casually performed. It is simply a case of mutual agreement between the boy and the girl and their parents. There is sometimes, but not always, a small family party where the couple is given blessings, along with much advice from parents and grandparents. Then follows the "zapoi" — a formal announcement of the intention to wed, which takes the form of another party, large or small, depending upon individual taste and the pocketbook. After this, there is a period of preparation ranging in time from a few days to a matter of weeks, depending again upon the individuals concerned.

No clergyman, nor other qualified person, officiates at the actual marriage ceremony. The bride, groom, and parents simply make public statements of their approval and the pair are Mr. and Mrs. This rite is held twice — first at the home of the bride's people, where advice and blessings are bestowed by her relatives; and then at the groom's parental home with similar proceedings from his family's members. There is no marriage certificate, no registration, no official record of any kind. The couple does not take up housekeeping in a home of their own; the bride moves her possessions to the groom's "house" in his parents' village, and proceeds to help in the communal kitchen, and in the fields.

Divorce, though not common, is a casual reversal of the marriage proceedings. Both parties agree to become divorced, the man returns his wife to her parents, the marriage is ended, and that's that.

WEDNESDAY, FEBRUARY 5

Went to Lipinski's last night but saw neither Joe nor Elsa, were not invited in, and of course walked home. Bah!

THURSDAY, FEBRUARY 6

Even the heroic efforts of our little heater have failed to warm the cockles of Pictin's water pipes sufficiently, so we are now forced to melt snow for even our drinking water. I have never been so perpetually thirsty in my life. Each mouthful of this horrible substitute gags me, yet I hang incessantly over the bucket and gulp the revolting potion.

Neither have I ever seen laundry pile up so relentlessly, nor in such awe-inspiring stacks.

This evening we decided that, water or no water, we would have to get at it, so after school we began the chore of hauling snow. We set the washtub close to the hall heater where the melting process would be faster, and then started our bucket brigade. We carted pailful after pailful of snow up to that greedy tub and watched each brimming pailful dissolve into a couple of spoonsful of water. How can so much snow make so little aqua? We finally gave up in disgust after lugging twenty-eight buckets of snow. The tub was three-quarters full, which wasn't enough for both washing and rinsing, so we washed sketchily, being careful not to use much soap, and rinsed not at all. The clothes are not dazzling in their whiteness, but at least the darn things are out of the way and not lurking on the floor in piles, waiting to trip us in the dark.

Mrs. Vereshagin arrived with Polly this evening in a state of great excitement. She had received a letter from the oft-pursued lawyer, and wanted it read and explained. He informed her, as we had, that since her marriage was not recognized by law, she was ineligible for the Widow's Pension for herself, but that she could apply for a seven dollars' monthly allowance for each child. Polly repeated this information to her mother in Russian, whereupon Mrs. Vereshagin was transported into the throes of ecstasy. Grinning and gesturing, she babbled on and on at Polly, who in turn grew wide-eyed, and then burst forth, "Geeweez, teachers, and now we gonna be reech! Eh-h-h-h, how reech we gonna be!"

Overcome at the prospect of this sudden wealth, they clattered off down the stairs, Mrs. Vereshagin calling back a dozen times, "E-h-h-h, spusi! Spusi hospidi!" and Polly in English, "Thank you! Thank you vyery moch!"

MONDAY, FEBRUARY 10

Tena Masloff arrived this evening to say that her father was ill, and could she have some pig butter. It took us some time to realize that what she wanted was lard for, we gathered, a poultice of some sort. We gave her half a pound and she went happily home.

Lard, being an animal product, is as fiercely frowned upon as meat, but when the occasion demands — or they think it demands — the sinfulness of forbidden fruit is forgotten.

We have stopped tossing our meat under beds and cushions when we hear a knock at the door. The Doukhobors disapprove of meat-eating (they say) but we are not Doukhobors — yet. And anyway, they do a number of things of which *we* disapprove! Besides, we've seen countless Doukhobors in restaurants in town, gorging on rare steaks, and gulping sausages.

THURSDAY, FEBRUARY 13

We were so weary yesterday that it seemed unlikely that school would ever let out. We had been to Castlegar the night before and since the recent thaw earlier this week, the road is a sea of melting snow and slush, and walking in it is a monstrous task. When we got home, we had coffee and a couple of hours of Scarlett, and it was 2 a.m. before we went to bed. So — we were ready to collapse by three yesterday afternoon, and all decided to go up and have an hour's snooze before supper. It was my turn to prepare the evening meal and I was amazed, when I awoke, to see that it was pitch dark. I reached for my flashlight and migosh! my watch showed twenty minutes after eight! I had slept for five hours . . . supper was 'way late . . . I leaped out of bed, lit fires and lamps, and scrambled about getting a quick meal ready.

When I called them, Peg and Gertie appeared, sleepy and befuddled, and we sat down to eat. Peg asked, "What time is it?" and I replied, "Oh, I don't know — about nine o'clock, I guess. I couldn't believe my eyes when I woke up and saw it was twenty after eight. What a glorious sleep!"

Gertie glanced at her watch and then said, "Well, for the first time in my life, I'm eating supper at 4:30 in the morning!"

Peg and I were puzzled at first, but a good look at our watches corroborated Gertie's statement. It was 4:30 a.m. In my drowsy state I had mistaken twenty to four for twenty after eight, so supper was somewhat more than fashionably late last night. But it was lovely to get up from the table and go back to bed again until seven. We may even revise our schedule permanently.

TUESDAY, FEBRUARY 18

Early last evening, Bill Zarikoff and Paul Lactin came up and asked, "And teachers, would you like to go to dyandy funeyral? And you would like, we weell take."

We had no overwhelming desire to go to any funeral, dandy or otherwise, but agreed that it would be interesting to see just what takes place at a Doukhobor funeral, so we thanked the boys and went with them over to the Shukin village, where the grandfather Shukin had died on Sunday.

As we went up the path to the house, I thought there surely could be no funeral in progress there. A dozen or so children were playing in the wet snow, chasing one another and screeching and squabbling at the tops of their voices. But then, I reasoned, children do not realize the significance of a funeral. But on the porch, and in the doorway, groups of young people jostled and shoved one another, and giggled and laughed, and chewed gum with loud popping noises, and crack-crunched-ptoo-ed sunflower seeds. There was no funereal air there either. They moved aside to make way for us, and we entered the big front room. Quite a number of people, all older folk, were gathered there. They were in small groups, some praying, some chanting dolefully, others gossiping happily — but all bowing deeply to one another.

At the end of the room, near the table set with the usual bread, water, and salt, the old widow sat weeping and rocking gently back and forth in her grief. Beside her was the coffin, a rough wooden box, and in it sat the corpse, propped up at a sixty-degree angle, gazing woodenly at the mourners! It was such a startling experience to suddenly and unexpectedly find ourselves staring into that cold, dead face that we were able only to gather enough wits to go and indicate our sympathies to the widow and then depart in haste. So we have no further knowledge of Doukhobor wakes — I suppose that this ceremony would be called a wake.

This morning, while school was in session, the procession went by on its way to the little burying-ground down by the river. The chanting mourners walked along behind the horse-drawn sleigh which carried the coffin — and there the corpse still *sat!*

Six weeks after the funeral, there is a memorial service. At the end of that time the soul, which has been wandering about trying to reach those it has left behind, goes to its reward in the life hereafter. Yearly memorials are held on the anniversary of the death.

THURSDAY, FEBRUARY 20

As on two previous occasions since moving in here, we ate breakfast this morning with the windows wide open to the gale, comforters wrapped around us, and our eyes streaming copious tears.

The pipe of our cookstove makes its way to the chimney by way of a devious and highly complicated route. It first parts company with the stove through a hole in the wall, and then ambles haphazardly around with no less than four elbows, before it finally takes the path of least resistance and gropes for the chimney. Halfway along its tortuous trail it is joined by the pipe from the hall heater. All this makes for very poor draught and a monstrous accumulation of soot in the pipes, with the result that the smoke, instead of easing out the proper vent, comes pouring into the room in choking billows. So it is a case either of breathing for awhile and then freezing to death, or of being moderately warm for a quarter of an hour and then suffocating. Whatever our choice, we haven't a fighting chance at survival anyway. Therefore, we have to take the only other alternative, which is to pull down all the beastly pipes every couple of weeks, cart them down the stairs, dump out the soot (which invariably blows all over our washing on the line), and tote them back up again. Getting the confounded things back in their proper order, so that they point finally towards the chimney instead of in the direction of my bedroom door, or towards the stairs, entails much brainwork, thirty-seven clamberings on and off chairs, many gored fingers, and several off-color words.

MONDAY, FEBRUARY 24

To encourage cleanliness and good health habits, we each have morning health inspection with the pupils taking turns at being "doctor" and "nurse." In order to attain a star for the day, each youngster must present clean face and hands, combed hair, and a clean handkerchief. Sam Zaitsoff, in Gertie's class, has for weeks fished the same immaculate, neatly folded handkerchief out of his desk at inspection time, but to-day he was minus this badge of perfection and so could not have a star. Gertie said in surprise, "Why, Sam! What happened to you to-day? Where is your handkerchief?"

He replied sullenly, "And I took eet home."

"But why?" asked Gertie. "No handkerchief, no star."

"Wyell," Sam mumbled, "and fawder-my is asking eef I am using da hankychif and I say no and fawder-my say eef I don't using eet, den here's no use, so he say breeng home da hankychif."

WEDNESDAY, FEBRUARY 26

While getting dressed for school this morning, I thought I heard someone enter the downstairs hallway. Surmising that it was a much-too-early pupil, I intended to call down the stairs and tell him to play outdoors for awhile. Clad only in the first two basic items of a gal's attire, since I knew I wouldn't be seen from below, due to the turn in the stairs, I opened the door — and there stood old Mike gazing at my midsection. As quickly as THAT, I had opened the door,

gasped, and slammed it shut. But daunted not at the sight of a near-nude pedagogue, Mike opened the only barrier betwixt me and shame, and croaked, "E-h-h, wot's da myatter? No myatter, meessus — you cawvered!"

I suppose he's seen many a nude parade in his time and this is old stuff to him, but me, I just can't enjoy prancing around in public clad only in panties and bra.

Mike was desperate for the medicine purchased in Nelson on Saturday, and when he had dumped his vegetables onto the floor he collapsed into a chair, closed his bleary old eyes, and rocking back and forth went into his usual routine of wheezing and gasping and "oh-h, hospidi, hospidi — ah-h-h - whee-e-e-e - oh-h shyit."

I had by this time donned clothing more suitable for company and joined Gertie and Peg, who were as sure as I that this time Mike's demise was surely in the offing. Peg tossed a pill into his gaping mouth and, much to our relief, his groans and wheezes began to subside. After a few more minutes of rest, he wavered to his feet, preparing to leave, and I saw that another button was gone. That leaves only one more. Oh dear!

THURSDAY, FEBRUARY 27

Mrs. Lipinski didn't have our package ready when we called last night, so she had to ask us in to wait for it. She wasn't speaking to Elsa, and Elsa wasn't wasting any words on Joe, so it was a rather strained interval, with Mr. Lipinski striving to be jovial in such an icy atmosphere, and Joe trying to be quietly polite. It's quite obvious that too many cooks spoil the broth, and that a stitch in time would have saved four — from misery.

MARCH

SUNDAY, MARCH 2

WE'VE invested in a small battery mantel radio so now we'll know some news more recent than that of the Riel Rebellion, and the words of later songs than Old Kentucky Home.

MONDAY, MARCH 3

Pete Savinkoff, in the primary grade, has no talent for reading. Pete, as a matter of fact, has no aptitude for anything much. He is a long, gangly child with droopy eyes and a mouth always agape, with his tongue lolling out. To-day he stumbled and mumbled through his reading as usual, chanting, "Lit-tle . . . Boy . . . Bl . . . Blue, come blue . . . come . . . come . . . Little Boy Bl . . . Blue, come bl . . . blow your . . . come blow y-y-your . . ." and Peg, in exasperation, cried, "Oh, sound it, sound it!"

Joyfully, Pete read breezily, "Come blow your sounditsoundit."

FRIDAY, MARCH 7

If the roads get any worse, we'll have to buy a canoe to get to the bus. There are huge pools, some shin deep, and we have either to wade through them or walk extra hundreds of feet around them. It seems impossible that there can be any shortage of water up here in the sunmertime, for right now it is a case of water, water everywhere.

But the buds are beginning to swell, and to-day we saw a robin. Also, we hear marbles rattling in the boys' pockets — than which there is no surer sign of spring.

TUESDAY, MARCH 11

At recess Gertie and I heard a commotion outside and upon investigation found a terrific fist fight in progress between John Ozeroff and Billy Reibin. The Doukhobors are "agin" militarism, fighting, war, army and navy, airforce, and anything else that has to do with aught but pacifism; except, that is, when it comes to good neighborly knock-'em down quarrels, and that is a horse of a different color. In a squabble with his neighbor — or uncle, or brother — it is permissible, and fitting, for Pete to bash Mike a series of good ones and for Mike to retaliate in like kind, especially if Pete should happen to be looking in the other direction.

That was the sort of struggle that was going on this morning when Gertie and I flew out to separate the pugilists. We held them, still snorting and clawing at the air, and tried to find out what had started the fracas.

"And Meess Hulls," John blustered angrily, "Beelly peess in my eye."

Billy tried to lunge at John again and sobbed, "And I was in da toilet, and I was peessing, and John was looking, so I gave heem in da eye!"

Gertie swallowed a gulp of laughter and turned her back to view some object far off up the mountain. I scolded, "Now, no more of this. Do you both hear me? You should be ashamed of yourselves — fighting like this, and talking that way! Stop it at once, both of you."

Billy grumbled, "And eef he ees looking any more when I am peessing . . ."

Gulping, I intervened, "Alright now, that will do. That's — stop it — you — John, you stop looking, and — and — Billy, you stop p . . . now that's enough of this nonsense!"

And then the blessed relief of going inside, out of sight, and laughing until our sides ached. Oh, just wait till we tell *this* one to our friends in town! Oh-h-h, hospidi, hospidi!

THURSDAY, MARCH 13

Walter Stroogoff has apparently long been smitten by Peg's charms for to-day his mother came on a strange mission. She is one of the very few women who knows a little English, and how she did use it this afternoon!

She arrived shortly after Peg had dismissed her class and presented her with a doily before breaking into the preliminaries, thus: "And Walter-my vyery good boy, huh, Barclee?"

Not having any idea of what was in the air, Peg was politely enthusiastic and agreed that yes, Walter was a fine boy. Mrs. Stroogoff continued, "And vyery strong is Walter, eh-h-h, how beeg and strong!" Peg said that yes, indeed Walter looked like a strong, healthy young man.

"And you like my boy Walter?" the visitor pressed on.

Peg walked right in. "Oh yes, I like Walter fine," she said.

Mrs. Stroogoff beamed from ear to ear as she jumped in for the kill.

"Ah-hah! Might you like cookum, eatum, shleepum Walter?"

Pegs says loftily that she is now on an equal footing with me, but I contend that my proposal(s) was/were much more romantic. At least *my* Lochinvar, in each case, did his own asking.

But Peg has another feather in her cap. When unpredictable Mrs. Tarstabitoff is favorably impressed with her, she tenderly calls Peg "Barclitchka."A girl named Hopka, when a toddler, is called "Hopitchka"—a little-girl pet name, as we would change Catherine to Cathy, or Dorothy to Dolly. When she marries, Hopka becomes "Hanya." In this way, little Marhutichka becomes Marhutka at school age, and Marhunya when she marries. So, since Peg is quite small,

103

Mrs. Tarstabitoff in a good mood refers to her as "Barc-litchka", or in other words, "Little Barclay."

I had to remind the gloating Peg to-day that when Mrs. T. is annoyed with her, she exchanges "Barclitchka" for "sootchka" — which is Russian for bitch.

FRIDAY, MARCH 14

Polly Vereshagin, breathless and windblown, came crashing into school this morning before anyone else had arrived, and joyfully reported that "da monya" had come.

"Eh-h-h-h, how moch monya! And twenty-eight *dollars!* And now every mawnt' we're gonna gyet like dot moch monya! And to-day mawder-my weell go Nyelson and buy la-awtsa t'eengs! E-h-h, how lawtsa she weell buy!"

She will, too. But nothing that her poor scrawny little urchins need.

MONDAY, MARCH 17

This morning, at a little after six, we were awakened by the most outlandish banging and thumping on the outside door. Peg staggered down to see what it could be at such an ungodly hour — surely there must be a tragic emergency! — and opened up to find Johnny Hrukoff dangling goggle-eyed, in the grasp of his father on one side, and his grandfather on the other. Parent and grandparent were seething with rage and exasperation and ordered Peg to "breeng Meess Meelin, hurryop!"

When Gertie went down, Mr. Hrukoff the younger beseeched her, "And Meess Meelin, you weell shtrap John? He is vyery byad boy and dossn't leestens to os wot we tyell heem. And here, you shtrap for os!"

They didn't tell us *that* at Normal either — that it would be our lot to punish pupils for offences committed at home. And especially a pupil who would be dragged to school by a great hulking pair of grownups each three times his size. And particularly at 6 a.m. It really begins to appear that those wise instructors at Normal were remiss in a great many details.

But perhaps the male Hrukoffs recall the time that Gertie
did strap the foul-mouthed young Johnny most soundly, and
with gratifying results — for a few days. They know that

105

she can, and will, use the strap when it is called for. On that occasion, however, she was rewarded by a visit from the distaff side of the family, in the persons of Johnny's mother and grandmother, both of them screaming Russian oaths and shaking their fists at her. As they left, Mrs. Hrukoff's parting threat was, "And you wait, you sootchka, I gonna feex you. You see! I gonna styick knyife in your byack! You wait — I feex! Sawmetime dark, I gonna feex you! Ptui!"

In that instance the Hrukoffs apparently didn't approve of corporal punishment.

Mrs. Hrukoff in a rage — or, for that matter, out of one — looks as though she could ably play the role of murderess any old day in the week, so Gertie trod the precarious path of trepidation for some little time. And Mrs. Hrukoff's sister added small comfort to Gertie's frame of mind when she came over to tell her, "No myatter, you no scyare, Meess Meelin, my syister cryazy. She not do nawting. She cryazy in her hyead. All-a-time she do cryazy t'eengs. You no scyare."

FRIDAY, MARCH 21

Those who are supposed to know such things have decided that our lives are of no great consequence, I guess, for our guard has been relieved of his duties and we now live with PERIL, according to our friends. Or perhaps it is because the authorities feel that since this school is right in a village, there is little likelihood of an attempt being made to destroy it. We believe that this last is the case, and are not concerned for our safety. But we do have fun in town telling everyone how we creep insecurely from dark to dawn, never knowing when we'll wake up to find ourselves hurtling through space, or battling our way through searing flames. As we make our exit, we hear their outraged protests: "My dear, it's just not right that those poor girls should have to live in such dreadful fear. Why, you only have to look at them to know that they're on the verge of nervous breakdowns."

106

Sometimes, for variety, we are very blase about the whole thing, and when they exclaim at our bravery we shrug our shoulders and scoff nonchalantly, "Oh heavens, it's nothing!"

Then they say admiringly, "My goodness, the courage of young people! Just look at those girls — as unconcerned as they can be!"

It's all very satisfying to us because whichever way we choose to play it — desperate fear, or amused unconcern — we're always sure of being the objects of unbounded admiration, and the centre of attraction. Us and the monkeys at the zoo.

TUESDAY, MARCH 25

While at breakfast this morning, we saw the colossal Antifaoff grandmother waddling by. Suddenly she stopped, spread her feet, hoisted her voluminous skirts six or eight inches off the ground, and stood there with a beatific expression on her broad face. After a few seconds — just long enough — she dropped her skirts and continued on her way.

"Well," mused Peg enviously, "there's one thing about it — that method certainly saves a lot of time and bother."

THURSDAY, MARCH 27

The children have started attending Russian school at 3:30 each day. These classes were just begun last week, much to the disgust of the girls, who go only because they have to, and to the delight of the boys, who go only to have a rip-roaring good time. They are the despair of their teacher, who comes over on his bicycle from Castlegar every day, and who should rightfully tan their britches. The din issuing from the "bibliotika" — meeting house — while Russian school is in progress, is comparable to the racket of a combined barnyard and Ladies' Aid meeting, and whenever we hear it, in passing, we are thankful that at least we have discipline, if nothing else.

FRIDAY, MARCH 28

Another week before Easter vacation! And by the time the holiday is over, the road should be dried up and the hike up here won't be so tiring. The grass is beginning to show little green spikes, and the phoebes are calling plaintively to one another. The water is on again in the Pictin kitchen, and we now have to carry the buckets up only one flight of stairs — and e-h-h-h, but spring is wonderful!

The air is awhir with skipping ropes, and we listen to the girls chanting over and over as they jump —

"A-a-a HOUSE to ryent, apPLY weedEEN —
W'en POLLY goes out for DRYEENKing geen,
For DRYEENKing geen ees a VYERY byad seen —
W'en POLLY goes out, den MYARY cawmes een.
A-a-a HOUSE to ryent, apPLY weedEEN —
W'en MYARY goes out for DRYEENKing geen,
For DRYEENKing geen ees a VYERY byad seen—
W'en MYARY goes out, den NYELLIE cawmes een.
A-a-a HOUSE . . ."

108

APRIL

TUESDAY, APRIL 1

THIS is April's Fool Day, but I don't think this evening's occurrence had anything to do with the date. It was wash-night again and we were busy slopping away at the hateful chore, door and windows open since it was a lovely balmy evening.

What with the clatter of our work and the noise of the radio, we heard no other sound; but Gertie, in the midst of wringing out a sheet suddenly gave forth a queer little squeak, and Peg and I looked up to see her standing motion-less, gaping towards the door. And well she might squeak and gape — for there was John Argotoff! He must some-how have escaped from his corral, or chain, or whatever — and there he was, standing in our doorway, the one exit — except for the ropes — from this top floor.

He stood wavering from side to side, his hands dangling at his sides with, in each, a large rock. He leered insanely at us, saliva running from his twitching mouth, and then con-centrated on the gas lamp. Up to this moment, we had all stood there frozen, but when he shakily raised one arm as though to heave the rock at the lamp, we suddenly came to life. Peg grabbed the broom, and Gertie and I scrambled for sticks of wood, upsetting the washtub in our frantic haste. We converged upon the poor wretch, waving our weapons and yelling, "Go! Get out! Get out! Stupi! Go."

109

Weak with relief, we watched him slowly turn and fumble his way down the stairs and then go loping, ape-wise, up the road. He had not gone far when he was met by his little sister, Fannie, who must have been sent out to look for him. She slapped him on the backside, jabbered at him in Russian, and taking his hand, dragged him off into the dusk, and home—we hope!

This was one of the worst moments yet, and if I have any choice in the matter, I'll take a carload of bombs in preference to another visit from wobbling, drooling John. Imbecility, I have always felt, never before having witnessed it firsthand, is something to be terribly pitied. But when it is at such close range as it was to-night, it is stark horror and there is no room for compassion in one's mind — at least, not in *this* one's, I'm ashamed to say.

And Peg and Gertie agreed as we got down on our clacking knees to mop up the water that lay in pools over the entire floor. What we would have done, had John not turned to the stairs, we have no idea. I do know that one little spurt of bravery was the only one I possessed, and how can I ever face anything again with only these quivering stalks of jelly to hold me up?

"Yes, but," quavered Gertie, "won't *this* be something to tell in town? Oh-h-h boy!" And suddenly we felt much better.

THURSDAY, APRIL 3

To-morrow is Good Friday and the beginning of the holidays, so this afternoon we had planned, as a surprise, to give all our pupils Easter eggs and candy. In view of the Hallowe'en, Christmas, and Valentine handouts, they would apparently have been more surprised if we'd had no gifts for them, because as soon as they came in after lunch, Nicky Stoochnoff put up his hand and asked in his deadpan, matter-of-fact way, "And w'en you weell geeve da Easter presents?"

Peg was so annoyed at his *expecting* something, and so disappointed at having her surprise spoiled, that she said

she felt like eating all the goodies herself and asking him
coldly, "What Easter presents?"

We had bought for each one a chocolate egg decorated in
the usual fashion with a candy flower and the pupil's name.
Never before had they beheld such wonders and we were
repaid a dozen times when we heard the squeals of delight
and the choruses of, "E-h-h-h, how ni-ice! How preetty! How
lawvely! E-h-h-h, how you got like dis eggs?"

Even Nicky, who would have preferred firecrackers at
Hallowe'en, broke down and exclaimed, "E-h-h-h, how ni-
ice!" when he received his treasure.

And so we're just about ready to leave. On our way to the
bus we can decide just how to present our account of John's
visit. Since the passage of a couple of days it doesn't seem
quite so terrifying, and Peg is inclined to think that the
Amused Attitude would be most effective. But Gertie and I
feel that the Scared to Death version would go over better
and would get the most satisfying reactions. And really,
that one would be a lot easier to do!

SUNDAY, APRIL 13—In Town

Well, it looks as though we missed a chance to try out
those ropes in earnest. Last night, ten schools and halls were
burned down, and Ootischenia was bombed. Our town friends
are really on the rampage this morning — "Good gracious,
what if it had happened one night later? Those poor girls
would have been back there from their holidays and IN THE
BUILDING!"

The inspector is taking us out early to-morrow morning,
since reports indicate that the damage was too severe for us
to sleep there to-night.

MONDAY, APRIL 14

We've been out to Ootischenia and are back in town for
a few days until repairs are made to the schoolrooms and
our living quarters.

111

Peg's classroom is intact, since the only bomb tossed was at the Pictin half of the village; but a fair job was done there. The verandah, which extends the full width of all the Doukhobor houses, was blown off completely, and the roof over it is shattered and sagging. Every window in the building was blown out and the floors, upstairs and down, are littered with broken glass, wood splinters, crumbled plaster, and thick layers of dust. It is an indescribable mess, and we were glad to leave and postpone the grimy job of cleaning it all up. Workmen have been instructed to repair the verandah roof, and to put in new windows, but it appears that we are to be the charwomen who will do all the rest.

A guard appointed from Nelson, goes on duty to-night. Maybe they will order another strand spliced into our ropes, too!

TUESDAY, APRIL 15

We're famous! Pictures of the three of us, as well as of the blasted (double meaning here) school, grace this morning's paper. I think a bombing must be superior to a burning, because neither the schools which were burned, nor their teachers, made the papers.

FRIDAY, APRIL 18

Flash! Our pictures are in a Calgary paper as well! A copy arrived this afternoon from a friend there. I'll bet he's going around saying, "Lookit! I *know* that girl!" Knowing a notable will make him notable, too. Why, this thing could go on and on, and bring pleasure to no end of people — especially us. We're enjoying this prolonged holiday tremendously.

Our inspector chauffeured us out from town this morning and we arrived at 8:30, ready to literally pick up the pieces. All our pupils were on hand, so we were instructed to call the roll, and then dismiss them so that we could get our quarters back in order.

The schoolrooms had been hoed out, but upstairs the mess remained as it had been a week ago, only a little more so, since the window-putter-inners had been clumping around through the plaster and glass for several days, and had thoughtfully dropped gobs of putty here and there, and then clumped some more.

We tied up our hair, donned old slacks, gritted our teeth, and dug in. We pushed, pulled, scraped, grubbed, and swept, until there was more dust in the air than can be found in a prairie dust storm, a flour mill, and a sideroad, all combined. Our complexions gradually changed from drug store Rosy to Ghoul Grey, and when our upper and lower teeth met, their union felt like it sounds when you scrape two pieces of sandpaper together. We were at it from ten o'clock this morning until five-thirty this afternoon, with time out only for lunch, which consisted of glass-filled sandwiches, splinter tea, and cake frosted with plaster. But now our walls, furniture, floors, windows, and curtains are all sparkling clean, and we scarcely recognize the place since even *before* the blast. It just might be possible that a bomb here, say about once a month, would be a darned good idea!

We have a myan right here in our myidst! He is our guard, whose name is Nolan, and who informs us that he sleeps in the spare "house" opposite our storeroom. He is sixty-fivish, not too immaculate, and gifted with the wagglingest tongue I have ever heard.

At dusk, he took up his position in Gertie's classroom, his huge gun across the desk, his head cocked, and his ears attuned to skulking would-be bomb-setters. Every half-hour or so, he shoulders his musket, sentry-wise, and, looking like the re-incarnation of Daniel Boone, slinks stealthily around the village. He peers under rocks, behind grass blades, into water taps, and through knotholes — those being the most unlikely spots for a bomb to be crouching — and would, I am sure, run a mile if he heard a twig snap behind him. Or even in front of him!

WEDNESDAY, APRIL 23

Leaving everything in the trusty hands of Nolan, we

113

went on our weekly Castlegar-Lipinski trip last night. At Lipinski's, where we had to wait again for our eggs and butter, some reference was made to the bombing. Elsa, we felt, thought it would have been lovely if we three had gone up with it and come spattering down in ten thousand gory little pieces. Auntie looked at her charming niece-in-law, when she looked at all, as though she (Elsa) were a remnant of decomposed fish; and Joe, I think, is contemplating drowning both of them. Misery, 'tis said, loves company, so friend Misery should certainly not be lonely in that house. Mr. Lipinski is scarcely in evidence any more; he probably sits out in the peaceful barn with the soft-eyed cows who never bicker nor wrangle.

MONDAY, APRIL 28

Since breakfast this morning consisted of scrambled smoke and soot marmalade washed down with tears, we had to face the fact that it was once more time to drag the stove pipes down. We tried to be brave little Pollyannas and make the thought of the fiendish job deliciously tempting by setting it to music and warbling It's Pipe-Cleaning Time in Ootischenia. But that method of self-kidding is a fake, and anyway Pollyanna made me sick even when I was a child.

So we resumed our groaning and moaning, increasing the volume until Nolan heard us (at last!) and offered to do it this afternoon. Which proves something about the Pollyanna adage: if we'd been cheerful and uncomplaining, we'd have had to do it ourselves. By grouching, we evaded the filthy chore and, after inviting Nolan for supper as a reward, we trooped down to school praising Allah for the gift of Nolan, and wallowing with joy at having no truck with the odious business — we fondly thought.

When we went up after school, we walked into the most devilish mess ever accomplished by man or beast. It was obvious that dear, kind Nolan had made no slightest attempt to hold the pipes horizontally, for there were black smoochy streaks all over the floor where he had tramped back and forth with wet boots through little heaps of spilled soot. I would previously have defied anyone to produce any dirtier combination than soot and water sprinkled around together at random; but Nolan to-day achieved the ultimate — he had *swept*. He had laboriously shoved the broom round and round, and up and down, and in and out, and back and forth, until the whole grimy mixture was caked on the floor like clay. Then he had washed his hands of the whole kaboodle and gone to bed. I have heard people say that men are so handy at jobs around the house, but if Nolan is a man, I'll take a flock of chickens and a litter of pigs for mine.

We had to grub around on our hands and knees, and scrub, and carry clean water up, and pack dirty water down, and scrub, and scrub, and scrub. And then, as a glorious climax, to feed the monster!

To entertain an interesting guest is one thing; to be "entertained" by Nolan is another. He belongs to the hash-and-rehash school and intersperses every seventeenth word with "heavens t' Betsy." A simple remark like, "It's getting colder, isn't it?" sets Nolan off like this:

"Colder? Why, heavens t' Betsy, you don't know what cold really is. Say, I remember one spring — or was it fall? — no, it couldn't have been the fall because in the fall of that year, heavens t' Betsy, I was in Toronto. Or no, wait a minute now — maybe it was Winnipeg — lemme see — no, it was Toronto alright, because I was walking down Yonge Street. Well sir, you wouldn't believe it, but heavens t' Betsy, that morning — no, it was afternoon, because I remember I had clam chowder for lunch that day. Say, you never tasted clam chowder like they made at Joe's Place — or no, it wasn't Joe's Place either; it was — now what in the dickens did they call that little cafe? Tom's Place? No — no — it was — lemme see now — heavens t' Betsy, I should remember that name. Oh sure! Jim's Place, that was it, Jim's Place! Heavens t' Betsy, that Jim was the biggest Swede I ever see! Or he mighta been a Dane — or maybe a Norwegian. Anyhow, he was Scandinavian of some kind, but I'm pretty sure he was a Swede. And heavens t' Betsy, wasn't his clam chowder real clam chowder though! Now some folks don't put enough clams in their clam chowder. It's just like steak-and-kidney pie — why, heavens t' Betsy, some steak-and-kidney pie is all steak and no kidney. I sure go for the kidney — oh, I like liver and heart and all that other stuff too, but give me kidney every time. By gosh, that reminds me of a fellow I met once out in Hamilton — or was it in Calgary that George and I met? Lemme see now — no, by heavens t' Betsy, it was Edmonton because . . ."

This goes on and on and on, and, heavens t' Betsy, we never do find out what cold really is. It's only by saying, "Sh-h! Wasn't that a noise downstairs?" that we ever get rid of him.

But he's harmless, and means well, and, heavens t' Betsy, he's only trying to provide entertainment for us.

TUESDAY, APRIL 29

Mrs. Vereshagin has apparently received the first of the money promised her for the children's support. They arrived for school this morning dripping with, I am positive, the whole twenty-eight dollars' worth of useless trash—Woolworth rings, bracelets, necklaces, pocket knives, and pencil boxes, as well as piles of unnecessary scribblers.

All the pupils diligently fill every last line in their notebooks, and then rule the inside covers for use as well, because every book goes home for "fawder-my" to inspect, and if any space is left in it anywhere, it comes back to be filled before a new one is released. When everyone exclaimed over the Vereshagin stock of new scribblers, these children of wealth shrugged their bony shoulders and replied scornfully, "And dot's nawt'eeng, we're *reech!*"

In a lesson with grade four today about the gallivanting Columbus, I made some reference to the time when people did not yet know that the earth was round. Willie Polonikoff stared at me as though I had said that borsch is made in a spinning wheel, and asked in tones of deep disgust, "And who say like dot da eart' is round?"

Since it appeared that Willie had never heard of this rank foolishness, I tried to explain to him how geographers, astronomers, scientists, et al, had arrived at the knowledge and proven it. Willie snorted in amusement at the idle prattling of such dolts and, laughing heartily, scoffed, "Eh-h-h-h, *round!* Dis guys sawme kinda cryazy!"

"But, Willie," I tried to reason, "don't you think that maybe those great scholars know just a little more about such things than you do?"

He closed his scribbler, put down his pencil, folded his arms on his chest, and with haughty finality uttered his ultimatum: "And dot's not true. And I don't believe." Then he closed his eyes and, whistling under his breath, he simply ceased to listen to any more drivel.

I, too, once thought as Willie does but, unlike him, I hadn't the courage to say so, at least not in school.

WEDNESDAY, APRIL 30

Peg is at the end of her rope as far as Tena Rezansoff is concerned. When we combined classes in January, I bequeathed Tena to Peg not, I must confess, without rejoicing. Every day in the week, after instructions to color something blue and red, someone's hand goes up and a plaintive voice says, "And here got no blue crayon."

Peg asks, knowing well what's coming, "Well, where is it? You had a blue crayon yesterday."

The reply is invariably the same, "And Tena ate it."

Next day, the order is to make the three little pigs with plasticine, but, "And here got no plyasticine."

"But I gave you all new plasticine only last Thursday. Get busy and find it."

Tearfully, "And Meess Barclay, I cyan't. Tena ate it."

To-day came the ultimatum in Tena's voraciousness. She was wandering about with myriad streaks of red, blue, green, yellow, and black all over her face. Amazed at her piebald appearance, Peg exclaimed, "For goodness' sake, what on earth has Tena been eating now?"

Someone answered, "And I been sharpening my cawlored pyencils, and da sharpener was fooll, and I'm going to empty eet een da byasket and Tena don't lets to empty soch pretty cawlors, and she eats every byit in da sharpener."

We think it would be most interesting to view Tena's interior with its rainbow-hued digestive tract, and I wonder whether, should she ever have jaundice, she might come out in stripes or polka dots.

We were spared this week's walk to Castlegar. Nolan announced this morning that he was going over, and offered to bring anything we needed. We leaped at the chance and asked him to get us a roast — oh, between three and four pounds — "that is," I amended, "if it won't be too much to carry, along with your own things."

Nolan inhaled deeply, and exhaled thus: "Too much to carry? Why, heavens t' Betsy, I've toted as much as seventy-five pounds! Or, by gosh, I believe that pack was closer to seventy-*eight!* One summer when I was up north of Calgary — no, sir, it was further north than that! It was north of Edmonton, by gosh! The year I was in Calgary was before that, come to think of it. Heavens t' Betsy, but that's a long time ago. It's funny how you mix dates up sometimes. I remember . . ."

Luckily, it was time for the bell.

When Nolan got back, school was not yet out, so he just left the parcel on the kitchen table. When we went upstairs later, we were appalled at the huge chunk of meat he had bought. He came in to see whether we thought he had chosen a good roast (and possibly to see what his chances were for a meal) and, eyes bulging out of my head, I groaned, "Yes, it's lovely — but — why such a *heap* of it? This is certainly a great deal more than three or four pounds.

"Did you say 'pounds'?" he asked in surprise. "Why, heavens t' Betsy, I thought you said 'between three and four *dollars'!"*

Now we'll have to invite Nolan for supper not only tonight, as we had intended anyway, but a succession of nights, in order to get rid of this mammoth before it spoils.

But could it be just possible that our good friend knew what he was about? I wonder . . .

118

MAY

THURSDAY, MAY 1

THERE is an old legend which promises beauty and grace to maidens who, at dawn on May Day, wash their faces in the dew. We have nothing to lose, so last night we set the alarm for 5 a.m., and this morning at 5:15 were out groggily stumbling around in our pyjamas, slathering our faces with wisps of dripping, ice-cold grass. It was not so much our faith in the dew — or anything on earth, for that matter — bringing about a change for the better in our looks; but it would be so charming, years and years and years from now, we said, to tell our adoring grandchildren how, when we were young, we made the sweet, old-fashioned May Day quest for beauty.

But from now on, we'll buy our beauty at the cosmetics counter and to blazes with traipsing around in the soggy weeds before sunrise. All we accomplished was cold feet and sopping pyjama legs. And when I said, "Oh well, we can still fill our grandchildren with tales about how we used to wash our faces in the dew on May Day," Gertie dispelled all sentimental visions by replying, "Yeah, and at the moment you are smiling nostalgically into your lavender and old lace, your freckle-faced, tow-headed young snippet of a grandson will moan, 'Holy smokes, Gran, is *that* what happened to your face!'"

119

WEDNESDAY, MAY 7

For some little time, I have been having appendicitis twinges. My doctor has told me that I should part company with the obnoxious little hook, whose existence to-day lowered me to the depths of embarrassment by insinuating itself into a telephone call.

It was a glorious day, and when some of my pupils romped in after school and pleaded with me to come out and play tag with them, I shoved my books aside and escaped into the sunshine. To avoid being tagged, I ran up the porch steps — that is, I planned to run up the step — but tripped instead on the bottom one, which is concrete, and smashed my right foot into the riser with the force of a battering ram. It was terribly painful, and in the hour that followed my big toe assumed the proportions, and hue, of an eggplant. Suspecting that the toe was broken, I dispatched Mike Konkin to the station to phone my Dad and ask him to come out for me. I instructed him to say that I had hurt my foot and wanted to go in to the doctor.

"Be sure that you tell him *why* I want to go to town, Mike," I repeated.

Two hours later, a car came zooming into the village, stopped with a mighty screeching of brakes, and Dad came panting up the stairs followed by a trained nurse drooling with the joyful anticipation of a life-and-death race back to town.

"How is she? Where is she?" Dad asked me, who was sitting peeling potatoes right under his left eyebrow.

"What are you doing for her? Is she in much pain" hoped the nurse.

To Dad's relief, and R.N.'s disappointment, I soon had it all explained. Mike had, of course, without explaining why, only said to come out and take me to the doctor, and then promptly hung up. And poor Dad had assumed that the trouble was a command performance by my niggling appendix.

Never having met the nurse before, I felt like the boy who cried wolf, but was cheered up somewhat when I learned that this burlesque could have kept them rolling in the aisles for weeks if Dad's plans had not been thwarted. Convinced that I had a ruptured appendix, he had phoned for the ambulance! Thank heaven it was out!

Still . . . maybe I could have slipped the driver five to drive in like mad, with the siren screeching. I may never again have a chance at such a thrill and, after all, no one need have known that it was only an out-sized toe attempting to foil the Grim Reaper.

But I rode in most decorously, and Dad brought me back out to-night. I now boast splints on my toe — which was definitely broken — and hobble about in an old slipper of Dad's. Veddy, veddy stylish.

THURSDAY, MAY 8

My pupils are most solicitous, and pour sympathy over me by the bucketful. All but Willie Polonikoff, who has not yet forgiven me for siding with the dopes who say the earth is round. Willie said scornfully, "Eh-h-h-h, lookit! And she hyave styicks on her toe!"

MONDAY, MAY 12

Work has commenced in the gardens, and all the men and women toil daily from early morning until late at night, the men ploughing and the women raking, hoeing, and planting. They shout back and forth at one another like raucous crows, never happier than when they are at these dusty, back-breaking chores. The wheat sown last fall is quite high now, and its color is that beautiful, soft green of the rainbow. We awaken to sweet birdsounds and the cool, refreshing scent of the cherry blossoms beneath our windows. Ootischenia in May is truly beautiful.

SATURDAY, MAY 17

The splints are off my toe. Now, after a suggestion from Dad and another warning from my doctor, I have decided to be done with the appendicitis scare. So I have contacted a substitute teacher for the next two weeks, and on **Tuesday** morning the dirty deed will be perpetrated.

FRIDAY, MAY 30

'Tis all over. And I am finished with bed pans — for life!

I have received many letters from my young hopefuls, some of them true gems, as:

Dear Teacher —

If you aren't or if you are how are you in the hospitle? How are your appendiks? This one is quite a good teacher but you are the best teacher that I have ever known. And, glad to say I am all right and the rest of us except Mickey, who however is a little sick. He has a cold. We have started the story of Seasick the Sailor and Trampo the Traveller. It is an amazing story. I must close up now.

Yours truly,
Pete Salikin

P.S. This is just to remind you

Hope you a happy time,
And good holiday too,
For I know that you are
Very pretty, kind, and true.

*   *   *

Dear Miss Hulls —

We are all well hoping you all the same. I am very sorry for you. I hope you get better as soon as possible for we're missing you very much.

Dear Miss Hulls, we are trying to help this new teacher very much as much as possible. She is kind to us just the same as you did. So your to get better and come to us.

Yours sincerely,
Willie Polonikoff

(Apparently Willie has forgiven me at last!)

122

Dearest teacher,

In these lines I want to let you know that we are all well and hope you are the same. Miss Hulls, everyone fills sorry for you not coming to teach us and for your opration. Have you made your opration?

Miss Hulls, I saw you in my dream Sunday. You was very happy and teaching us. Miss Hulls, get better and come to teach us again. If you will be able, write for us.

Your pupil Nellie R.

*   *   *

Dearest loving Miss Hulls —

How do you feel before your operation? I hope you haven't much pains. Have you? I hope you the best luck I could ever think or get in the world. I hope you would come to us faster.

The new teacher is good. I like her very much but she isn't like you. I think I will have to close my letter now. Best wishes and good luck in the whole wide world.

Yours very lovingly,
Annie L.

Kisses to you from me

x   x   x   x   x   x   x

*   *   *

Very dearest teacher,

I am fine and hope you are the same. The new teacher teaches good. At first she didn't know nothing. We explained as much as we could. She is a good teacher. But as we are used to the work we always did she isn't. So it is like a knew school.

All is going on well. Most of all that we do is explaining. We almost ask no questions because she does not know them. We ask questions about only what she knows. I feel very sorry for you. We miss you very much.

Your school girl,
Polly B.

*   *   *

123

Dear teacher Miss Hulls —

I am writing you a first letter and I hope you will be satisfied with it. The first thing I will tell you is about our teacher, she is good except that she is not used to our school yet but I hope she will get along well until you are good.

Mary and I are helping her, Mary she is helping like giving out the blotters and pen points and I are giving out the goiter pills.

I hope you will be well again and as soon as the two weeks are past you should take off your clothes which you wear in the hospital, put on your own clothes and be good again.

Your scholar,
John R.

* * *

JUNE

MONDAY, JUNE 2

WAS received back into the fold with such glowing smiles of welcome that I feel guilty about all the times I've scolded and preached and ranted. Even Willie overlooks my foolish notions now that I have distinguished myself with an operation, for he asks sympathetically, "And how does your opyration hurts?"

WEDNESDAY, JUNE 4

Peg and Gertie went shopping without me last night. Joe asked politely how I was feeling and Elsa glared so ominously at him that the girls wished (for his sake) that they could report that I'd passed on to my reward, whatever it may be.

FRIDAY, JUNE 6

Annie Plotnikoff brought her year-old brother over after school to display his charms to us. Holding the baby by both arms, she demonstrated how well he could walk. As she guided his wobbly steps, she crooned lovingly, "Cawme on, cawme on. Walk, walk, you cyute leetle sawn of a beetch."

MONDAY, JUNE 9

Old Mike came wheezing up for more pills a little before 7:30 this morning. When he had swallowed one and the puffing, snorting, and praying had ceased, he asked plaintively, "Wot's da myatter you don't myarried?"

Our single status has long been the cause of much speculation, not only by Mike, but countless others of the Doukhobors. Here we are, twenty and twenty-one and still unmarried, which is unthinkable, and doubtless leads them to suspect that we are either lepers or hermaphrodites.

Gertie replied to Mike's query by saying off-handedly, "Oh, too busy. No time."

Mike sneered, "Eh-h-h-h, no time! You got time! You got time — lawtsa."

Since this reason didn't hold water, I tried my hand and said, "We can't. Nobody asks us."

This made more sense, and Mike livened up. "Shure!" he croaked, "*Shure* nobody askit. Nobody *gonna* askit, too! You too t'een — all you everytime too t'een! You like dot," and he made a circle with thumb and forefinger to indicate our girths. "Eh-h-h-h," he went on disgustedly, "too shmall, too t'een, no good. Man everytime like - it be - e - eg! Fyat! LAWTsa! *You* — ach! No good, no good!"

And, unable to bear the sight of such repulsive scrawniness a moment longer, he departed, shaking his head and clucking to himself.

WEDNESDAY, JUNE 11

We had Nolan to supper last night, and felt later that we deserved some compensation for our suffering. So at 11:30, just after he had made one of his rounds, we blew up paper bags and, turning the radio up to full volume, we crept noiselessly downstairs.

The door of the schoolroom was open on this warm spring night, and we could see him sitting by the coal-oil lamp looking at a magazine. We raised our bags and, after a silent 1-2-3, we popped them simultaneously with a terrific bang. Poor Nolan went straight UP into the air. Then he scrambled wildly for the door, rushed back to get his gun, and came tumbling out, wild-eyed — to make his getaway, I am positive. He was moving too quickly to see us in the dim light, but when he heard our gales of laughter, he stopped, looking very sheepish. But he rallied and laughingly said, "Y-y-you k-k-kids didn't fool me one bit. Heavens t' Betsy, I heard you coming down the stairs. I just let on that I was scared, and ran out like that t' let on that I didn't know it was just a trick. I didn't want to spoil your joke, is all."

We'd had our fun, so instead of contradicting him and spoiling his, we told our big, brave guard to come up for coffee. He accepted gratefully saying, "By heavens t' Betsy, that'll be real nice. I sure am thirsty."

"Thirsty?" I put in quickly, thinking that this was one time I'd try to wrest the floor away from Nolan. "Thirsty? Why, you don't know what thirst really means. I remember one time . . ." but Nolan drowned me out with, "By gosh, drinking coffee always reminds me of the evening — or was it the morning? Yes, I believe — no sir, it wasn't morning, either. It was evening, I remember now, because I'd been sawing wood all day, and I had a stiff arm for some reason or other. Sawing don't usually bother me none, but rowing now — heavens t' Betsy, but that's tough on the arms. I once rowed for two hours straight — I dunno but what it mighta been closer to two hours and a quarter — and let me tell you . . ."

Let him tell us? How is it ever possible to *not* let him tell us? When he had downed three cups of coffee and arrived at, "By heavens t' Betsy, them gallstones was the biggest I ever see," I whispered, "Listen! I thought I heard a noise downstairs," and Nolan reluctantly went off to his duties.

Peg said, "Noise? Why heavens t' Betsy, you don't know . . ." and Gertie and I shoved her head into the water bucket. That stopped her, and we went to bed wondering if similar tactics would also stop Nolan. But no, I think his Betsy would still come bubbling up from the bottom of the pail.

FRIDAY, JUNE 13

Olga Popoff went by to-day. We haven't seen her for some time now, nor have we heard anything further about her marriage; but it's obvious that a wedding would not have been amiss.

MONDAY, JUNE 16

Nick Pozdnikoff, whose father is on Piers Island, and Willie Polonikoff seem to be at loggerheads about something. They stood outside jabbering and scowling at one another, before school this morning, again at recess, and at noon hour and during school hours I saw Nick several times furtively shaking his fist at Willie. Since it didn't appear that their disagreement was serious enough for physical combat, I did not intervene, but when school was dismissed I watched to see whether there might be fireworks. As Willie followed Nick off the porch, he jabbed a penpoint into the enemy's most vulnerable spot and hooted, "Jump! Jump, Son of Freedom!"

At that, the fists went into action. I ran out quickly and collared them both, marshalling them back into the school-room for half an hour's detention. When the time was up, they went out peaceably enough but I heard Nick sneer, "Yah! And fawder-your eesn't on Pier's Island even!"

So much for fame and glory.

FRIDAY, JUNE 20

We had track events for our classes to-day. Everyone took a lunch and we went over to a cleared spot near the old barn school.

About halfway through the day, Mickey Shukin stumbled on the uneven ground and fell during a race. When he didn't get up, I ran over to him to see whether he had injured himself, or whether it was only his pride which had suffered. It was certainly not pride, for his left arm was doubled back from a point midway in the forearm, and the palm of his hand was almost cupped around the elbow. It was a most horrible sight, and frightened us all.

We sent one of the other boys to Castlegar on his bicycle to get the doctor, and took poor Mickey to our place. He was not in much pain, but very nervous and pale, and it was with great relief that we received the doctor when he arrived after what seemed an eternity.

He examined the patient and then said, "This arm should be set here and now," and turning to me, went on, "You look as though you could give him the anaesthetic if I direct you."

I felt all strength and color leave me as I envisioned to-morrow's headlines: BOY DIES UNDER ANAESTHESIA. TEACHER HELD.

But then I heard, as in a beautiful dream, "No, I don't believe I'd better do it here after all. He'd better go to Trail for X-ray first."

My heart began pumping again, and I came back from my cold, damp cell into the glorious sunlight once more. What a moment of horror *that* was! But now I can add one more experience to my repertoire: I am now full of the knowledge of how a suspect feels when he is acquitted of manslaughter.

MONDAY, JUNE 23

The first strawberries are ripe and the women are out in noisy, gaudy droves picking the luscious fruit, which goes to the local jam factory, across the railway tracks from the Brilliant station. The air around the plant is permeated with the heavenly aroma of hot jam, and as we passed there last night we decided to do down this evening and watch the jam-making process.

The building is a long, two-storied brick one facing on the railroad track for ease in loading cases of jam for shipment. Upstairs, where the preserving is done, we were amazed at the strict cleanliness; floors, tables, and workbenches are spotless and the workers, although not clad in any sort of regulation uniform, wear turbans or kerchiefs over their hair.

The huge, round-bottomed vats, suspended over fires, are of gleaming copper. Into each is dumped a twenty-pound pail of berries, and then twenty pounds of sugar, and nothing else. Brilliant-produced jam is pure jam, and not a hodge-podge of fifty percent fruit and fifty percent turnips and heaven-knows what! The cooked product is transported to a long room at the back of the building, where it is poured into cans, cooled, labelled, and packed.

The place was a madhouse as wooden pails bumped onto the floor, cans rattled, trucks clattered, scales jangled, and foremen shouted orders. What with the noise and the sweet fragrance of the rich jam, our heads spun as we went out into the cool, quiet night.

We had been given a little tin of the ruby nectar to sample, and we hustled home to find out, for sure, whether it tasted as wonderful as it looked and smelled. And indeed it did. Now that we've seen how clean everything is in the factory, and know how pure this jam is, we will surely always choose the Brilliant brand from grocery shelves from now on.

WEDNESDAY, JUNE 25

We have planned a little closing programme for Monday, the last day of school, and the youngsters have invited their parents to come and see the results of their year's work. They are setting up displays of writing, drawing, painting, handwork, and so on, and are almost as excited as they were before the Christmas concert.

Peg was at her wits' end as to what to do with Tena, and also Pete Masloff, since Tena has no accomplishments other than her appetite for crayons and plasticine; and Pete can only do two things; sit and look, and stand and look. However, they must perform, and since songs, plays, or recitations are far beyond either of them, Peg has had to devise an act for them out of thin air.

They, and six others, all bedecked with flowers, are to come in alternately, boys on one side and girls on the other, from opposite sides of the "stage." Each little girl curtsies to her partner, who makes her a formal bow, and then they all form a straight line at the back. That is all. Very simple and senseless, but it brings in both Pete and Tena who, I fear, are also quite simple and senseless.

A curtsy is—well, after all, it's just a—a curtsy. And a bow is merely a bow. But not to Tena and Pete. Peg has sweated for days on end trying to teach them. The boy behind Pete shoves him forward. Pete stands. The boy in front scowls and whispers loudly, "Cawme on, walk!" Pete walks. Peg says, "Bow!" Pete stands. Peg says, "Put one hand across your waist." He slaps a hand onto his stomach with a loud plop. Peg: "Put your other hand behind your back." The hand hangs limply over his buttocks. "Well, bow, Pete, *bow!*" Down he goes, head almost to the floor — and stays there. Peg directs, "Well, come *up!*" Up he comes. "Walk to the back," implores Peg. Someone leaves the line to come and get Pete and drag him back.

They go through the same routine, day after day, with Tena and her curtsy. To-day's rehearsal took exactly the same words and length of time as it did when they first tried it two weeks ago. Peg is tempted to get Tena into her curtsy and Pete into his bow, and then walk off and leave them petrified there. She's convinced that if she came back in a month's time, there would be no change in their positions until she yelled, "Well, come *up!*"

SUNDAY, JUNE 29

We didn't go home this weekend, for three reasons: we'll be finished to-morrow; we had too many things to do here; and we wanted to see what went on down at Brilliant to-day.

This is Peter's Day, also called Burning of Arms Day, the anniversary of the date in 1895, in Russia, when Peter Vasilvich Veregin (Peter Lordly) decreed that every rifle, sabre, sword, and weapon of any kind, should be burned. This mass burning of arms was the Doukhobors' absolute and final renunciation of militarism, and an act of defiance against the brutal Cossacks. It also resulted, indirectly, in the migration of the Doukhobors from Russia to Canada, for it was in 1899, when the Cossacks had driven them to their last place of exile, that Leo Tolstoy prevailed upon the Czar to allow them to leave Russia. Canada was their haven of refuge. They brought with them their staunch refusal to bear arms and, after all these years, still commemorate on this day their fathers' act of fierce defiance.

Naturally, we did not expect parades, flags, nor bands — all of these being tabu, as militaristic — but since this is the

131

biggest day of the year for Doukhobors, we thought that it would compare with our first of July celebrations in the way of excitement and jubilation. Such was not the case. Their day had only one thing in common with any of our important holidays, and that was the crowd of people. They jammed the station platform and railway tracks, the yard of the community's office buildings, the area surrounding the jam factory, and every other foot of ground in the vicinity. They stood shoulder to shoulder under the blazing sun, listening to speeches delivered by community elders, each of whom mounted a chair when his turn came to address the throng.

Sometimes, between speeches, the multitude raised its mighty voice in mournful chanting unison, and it was after one of these hymns that Peter Veregin clambered up onto the chair. Perspiration streamed down his repulsive face as he stood in his rumpled black suit and screamed at his subjects. He bellowed and roared and waved his arms; his hair fell over his forehead in dark strings, and the veins at his temples stood out purple. An air of restlessness seemed to seep through the packed crowd, but they remained to listen to the ranting of this man for whom many, if not all, feel nothing but disgust and who to-day resembled nothing so much as a raving maniac. Not far from where we stood, a woman fainted and was dragged out of the crush for air. At this point we left, fearing the same consequence from the combined assault of the terrific heat and the dreadful screeching of Peter the Purger.

It was not until late this evening that we saw people plodding home from the events of this great day. I should think that it must be a relief to them to have the ordeal over with. But — who knows — perhaps they enjoyed it all. Except, to my way of thinking, the wild oration of Peter — and even the delegates to the Annual Convention of the Incurably Insane would surely be further sickened by that demonstration.

MONDAY, JUNE 30

The closing programme was attended by all the mothers, who laughed and jabbered continuously, and by all the babies, who babbled and squawked. There were only three fathers present, the rest being too busy to come.

Never were there any prouder parents than the mothers of Tena and Pete, who were jerked, pushed, pulled, and prodded through their number, as in rehearsals. Mrs. Rezansoff and Mrs. Masloff beamed and beamed, and looked disparagingly at the others, whose poor stupid offspring merely spouted recitations or sang dull songs. Before the bow-and-curtsy act was over, Tena had devoured one wild rose and three leaves from her crown of flowers, and was casting anticipatory glances in the direction of Pete's syringa collar.

When the work displays had been admired, and reports and prizes distributed, they all left, the children shouting, "And you weell cawme to os again nyext year?" and the mothers bowing and saying, "Spusi. Spusi hospidi."

They had been gone only a few moments and we were enjoying a post mortem of the afternoon when old Mike came puffing along. He was very angry. His nostrils quivered, and he shook his fist at us as he demanded, "And vwy you have concyert? Jesus Christ no have concyert! No good dis concyert! And vwy you do like dot?"

We were all dumbfounded at his rage, but finally I answered, "What in the world is wrong with a little concert? The mothers like to see their children do things like that, and all the children like doing it. What's the matter with you, Mike?"

He sucked in his breath and exploded with, "Ach! Concyert! Concyert! Alla time concyert. No good, I tyell you. Jesus Christ not hyave concyert — vwy *you* have concyert? Concyert no good! Ach — ptoo!"

And off he stomped. As he reached the verandah steps, something went *clink* on the floor and rolled into a corner. I bent to see what it was, and found a button. Then, with horror, I realized that this innocent little black disc marked the complete undoing of old Mike, and I felt a surge of relief that this was his last visit — for this year, at least — and further relief that he doesn't walk backwards . . . oh, my goodness! If I return next September, I shall certainly come armed with a gift of safety pins for old Mike.

Our supper was composed of the only two foods we had left in the house — plain boiled beans, and tapioca pudding (made with water, ugh! since we have no canned milk and have never been tempted to buy fresh milk here). This repast, though on the gummy side, should certainly have provided a few thousand calories, and may help to build us up to sufficient avoirdupois to rate proposals of marriage.

We went to bid farewell to Nolan, who looked truly sorry to see us go, and lamented, "Heavens t' Betsy, I sure hate to see you girls go. I've sure enjoyed knowing you all, and I'll be downright lonesome here without you — darn near as lonesome as one winter I put in when I was eighteen — or lemme see, was I only seventeen? No — no, by gosh I was eighteen that year because that was the year . . ."

We would have liked to let him have this one last fling, but we do want to get home before Thanksgiving, so we had to cut him short and make our escape.

The sun was setting as we trudged along the dusty road. Smoke curled up from chimney tops as women began preparations for the evening meal, and when we passed the various villages, children came running to the gates to wave and call one last exhortation to "cawme byack next year." The same old, bent grandmothers patiently prodded the same reluctant, tail-switching cows homeward, and gave us their toothless smiles and low "slavas" as we met.

We felt that we should say good-bye to the Lipinskis, but no one answered our knock and there was no sign of anyone around, so they must have all been away. We were just as glad, really, for recent calls there have not been very pleasant for anyone.

As we wait for the bus, I gaze out over the panorama of Brilliant spread below us, and add these last lines to my year's diary.

The countryside is lush and green and rich. Throughout the verdant fields and orchards stand the two gaunt and dreary houses of each village; yet even their harshness is somewhat softened now by the surrounding full-leafed trees and shrubs. The hillsides are creamy with aromatic syringa, and its perfume is heavy on the cool evening breeze.

Immediately below us, the Kootenay froths and roars between its restraining granite walls — but soon it will be soothed and quieted, for there, in the V of the hills, waits the circumspect Columbia, slipping noiselessly through his broader channel. He will silently take this renegade Kootenay and lead him in dignity and serenity to the great Pacific.

Dusk is falling now, and here and there the rosy glow of coal-oil lamps winks at us through the trees. The raucous shouts of children at play around the villages have ceased. Except for the whir of a nighthawk, all is silent. And beautiful. And yes — a little misty before my eyes.

It has been a year that I shall never forget. Who could? Whether I come back next term or not, memories of this year will provide many a chuckle for a long time to come, and I feel that I shall have something to tell my grandchildren after all!

A Backward Look . . .

I did go back to Ootischenia . . . and back again . . . and again . . . and again, for a total of five years in all. The strange thing was that, despite the frequent sense of futility, the inconveniences and annoyances, and yes, even often the hardships, I continued to be drawn to that "other world" — for so it truly seemed in those days. Perhaps what kept me there was the realization of how so little could mean so much to those deprived children and often to their parents as well. Probably some inner selfishness made me return year after year to the place where accomplishments, however small, seemed so big. Or maybe I was simply in a comfortable (*comfortable?*) rut.

During those years everything concerned with school remained unchanged; situations, ridiculous and impossible anywhere else, continued to arise and continued to astound, harass, challenge, and exasperate me. But the rewards were there too, in the form of my pupils' pleasure at the smallest things (and also in the form of never-ending gifts of plums when they were in season! And I often gave thanks to Allah that the season was short.)

The grandmothers patiently went on urging the moody cows along the roadside; the causes of the children's absences continued to be laid to the everlasting meetings, to stawm-aches, and to calf-poolling. The seasons came and went, as they do everywhere, but at Ootischenia they seemed to come only as dreary monotones — from dust to gray rain, to freezing temperatures and mountains of snow, to dingy slush, to mud, and eventually to choking dust again. There were, of course, more "swell funeyrals", and several weddings (but never Olga's), and the women relentlessly continued to "gyet." And the moaning of the nocturnal chanters drifted across the fields like echoes from a tomb haunted by noisy ghosts. As I recall it now, the only really perceptible change — and how gladly I witnessed it! — came in the acquisition by old Mike of a new pair of trousers. The momentous—and fortunate—purchase had been made by the time I returned for my second year and so my fears on that score were put to rest.

Depredations continued too; the senseless bombings and burnings and nude parades apparently staged by the dissenting Sons of Freedom went on and on, and were followed by the inevitable exasperating court sessions. The once lovely tomb of Peter Lordly was the target of repeated sacreligious bombings; the jam factory, from whence emanated those delicious aromas and the best jam in all of Canada, was destroyed by fire; and only last year incendiary fires levelled two of the villages close to the old site of School Pleasant. These tragedies struck the immediate Brilliant area. But economically, all of British Columbia has suffered as a result of the crimes, small and large, allegedly committed by the Sons of Freedom. In their dogged pursuit of a solution to their "problem" — whatever it is — they continue to ignore the laws of Canada and their own responsibilities as citizens, while at the same time they demand all the privileges. They are reaping the unenviable harvest of disfavor wherever they go and it appears now that more and more doors are being closed to them. In one sense they are to be pitied for they seem to have no real and dedicated Cause; yet are other people — and not the least of these the law-abiding Orthodox Doukhobors — to live forever in fear of their lives and homes? Can a government go on and on being embarrassed by the actions of irresponsible people? Can we hope that they will *ever* become assimilated? Will they never realize what harm they are doing, if not to the rest of society, then at least to their own children? One can only deduce that, unlike normal parents throughout the world, the Sons of Freedom do *not* want to provide what is best for their children; that is stable, secure home lives and loving consideration for their physical and mental welfare.

... And A Thrilling Revelation

SEPTEMBER 19, 1962

To-day I returned to Ootischenia once more. On this occasion I was not a teacher but a visitor after an absence commencing in 1938. How thrilled and excited I was to see all the changes that have taken place during those years!

The great wheat field, at whose edge School Pleasant once huddled so disconsolately, has long since become an airstrip for CPA and the road thence to Brilliant is hard-surfaced. To gain the larger area required by the airlines company the Pictin village (ah, that cradle hook! and the escape ropes!) along with two others, was demolished.

No longer do stooped grandmothers nudge the family cows along the dusty road; the highway from the airport on into the community is still thick with chalky dirt, but nary a cow did I see anywhere. And Ootischenia boasts a store! — what a boon that would have been to Hrunka, Marhutka and Hopka! In various stages of construction are many modern homes, replacing the ancient brick and wood houses which are gradually disappearing.

At homes where I called I was, with pleasure to me, at once remembered and most graciously received. My host in one instance was the son of the Mr. Pictin in whose house we three lived. I spent a pleasant hour with Mike and his kindly wife, Lucy, who gave me news of the present whereabout of many of my old pupils, most of whom have left Brilliant and are raising families in other centres, some not too far away, others at great distances. It was with considerable pride — and justly so — that the Pictins showed me their home: a pleasant cottage containing modern furniture and electric appliances, even to a handsome television set! A still better house is in the offing for them; they told me that the land is all being subdivided and they, like many others, are purchasing lots for homesites. Mike and Lucy have a beautiful car, 1962 vintage, as well as a truck which Mike uses in his daily journey to Trail where he is employed. They are proud, as well they might be, and happy in the progress they have made. And I am happy for them and for their neighbors whose lives have been lifted from the gloomy and depressing surroundings in which they once lived.

I found it sad, however, that one note of bitterness crept in to mar this otherwise bright picture. I was told at one home that the husbands and fathers must stand guard all night, every night, to protect their homes and families from the torches of the despised Sons of Freedom, not all of whom are on the present attempted trek to Agassiz. And I was bitter along with these good folk. This outrageous state of affairs — in this year of this century! And in this country!

What was perhaps my greatest pleasure came from my visit to the school (and wonderful, wonderful! three or four of the children were sons and daughters or nephews and nieces of my former pupils! One little blonde cherub bore such a striking resemblance to her aunt that I could have hugged her). I found no shapeless sacks on the girls, no plutoks, no weird trousers on the boys. At the sight of these gay youngsters in dirndls, jumpers and pretty dresses, saddle oxfords, T-shirts, blue jeans, and all the other styles of clothing dear to children's hearts, a lump arose in my throat (I must confess this) at the memory of a beautiful, dark-eyed little girl who sat in my classroom sobbing her heart out for "just wan Eenglish dryess." (Tannis, Tannis! they all have English dresses now, every last one of them!)

Names have undergone a vast change too. I do not doubt
that there is still the odd Polly, Tena, Nellie; and the occasional Pete, Mike, and Nick. But the names that their teachers called out to-day were Elaine . . . and Margaret . . . and
Linda . . . and June . . . And the boys answered to Robert . . .
Leonard . . . Wayne . . . Ronnie . . . !

No longer, their teachers told me, do the beginners come
to school tongue-tied with fright at their speech handicap;
to-day's first graders already speak English *before* they enter
school! — and what a blessing that must be for children and
teachers alike. The old accent lingers in some cases, though
not nearly as pronounced, and in many I caught not a trace
of it at all. Further, the offensive "and" which used to
preface every remark, and which was such a bugbear to us
in our attempts to teach better English usage, seems to have
disappeared altogether.

I took what some might term unfair advantage of the
children, but in my excitement at all the wonderful changes,
there were things I felt I must know; and the youngsters —
pleased, their teacher said, at having a visitor — seemed
happy to co-operate with me in this subterfuge of mine.
Making a game of it, I learned from a show of hands that
every family has a car and/or a truck (while I cannot recall
a single motor-driven vehicle when I was there). I think that
all hands went up at the mention of radio (and only we
teachers had a radio then). Most signified possession of a
television set, and refrigerators are common in nearly all
homes. There are, I found, several electric stoves (as compared with the former villainous old monstrosities and
cavernous brick ovens, and in the homes I visited I saw, if
not electric stoves, very modern white porcelain wood-burn-
ing ranges. I also noticed pretty curtains and drapes, convenient cupboards, chrome kitchen sets, chesterfield suites,
and comfortable occasional chairs. What a contrast to the
bare windows, and scarred wooden benches and tables, and
blackened shelves open to the dust and smoke!)

The children told me excitedly about their new school
under construction nearby and said, "It's going to have
everything in it — even *washrooms!*" (And not one said,

141

"Washrooms! Eh-h-h-h! how lawvely!") The present building is a palace compared with my old quarters in the Pictin kitchen but certainly it is badly in need of replacement. There is no plumbing and the once-familiar water bucket and enamel hand basins still hold sway, but happily they will soon be relegated to the trash pile as have been the miserable gas and coal oil lamps, replaced years ago by fluorescent lighting. And that fiendish contrivance, the hectograph pad, has had its day too; the Ootischenia teachers have not only a mimeograph machine (oh, happy day!) but a Gestetner as well.

Another innovation was evident in the appearance, during the afternoon, of the Public Health Nurse who holds a regularly scheduled baby clinic. Very shortly after her arrival, the young mothers of the community began coming in with their babies; and these were *babies,* not pale little bound mummies. And in their mouths? Not one nauseating "shoogar ryag!"

Since all students above the sixth grade are now transported by bus to high schools in Kinnaird and Castlegar across the river, there are only two classrooms at Ootischenia. These are under the supervision of Mr. Fillipoff and Mrs. Murray, both of whom live in Castlegar. I am most grateful to them for their gracious acceptance of my intrusion to-day into their classrooms, an intrusion which I was not able, at this time, to explain. The publication of my story will clarify for them the reason for my seemingly mysterious visit, and I wish them to know that without their kind and generous help, I could not possibly have gleaned so much information concerning the Ootischenia of to-day.

———

Ootischenia to-day! How the years have changed your once haggard face! You are happy, Ootischenia — happier than you or I could ever have dreamed possible. And part — indeed, *most* — of your happiness is due, I am convinced, to your having accepted the Canadian way of life. *Things* — material things, to be sure — have played a large part; but are we not all concerned with the acquisition of material things — whether for comfort, convenience, conservation of time, or for easier living? Your people are rapidly becoming assimilated, Ootischenia, and you are justified in being happy for them, and proud of them for having determined to live as good Canadians.

But ... can you not persuade the Sons of Freedom, also, to let themselves become settled, secure, respected ... and happy?